GRIPPING STORIES

Other stories by Mark Sbani

BORN FOOL
BLUE BEAR (CO-WRITER)
EIGG THE MUSICAL (BOOK-WRITER)

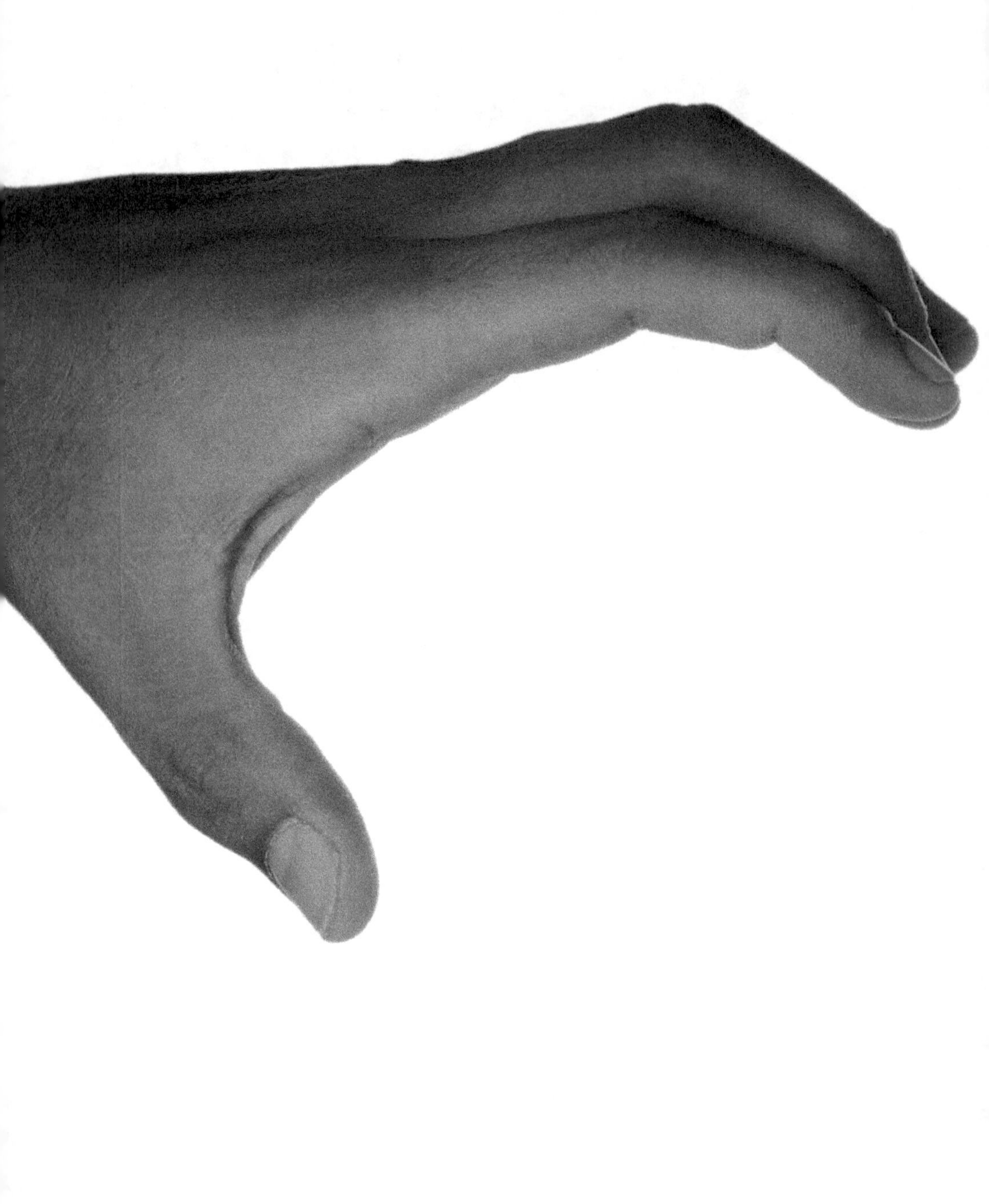

GRIPPING STORIES

MARK SBANI

marksbani@hotmail.com

1-2821976041 PAU4-197-821

1-14771272801 ISBN: 979-8-9987949-0-2

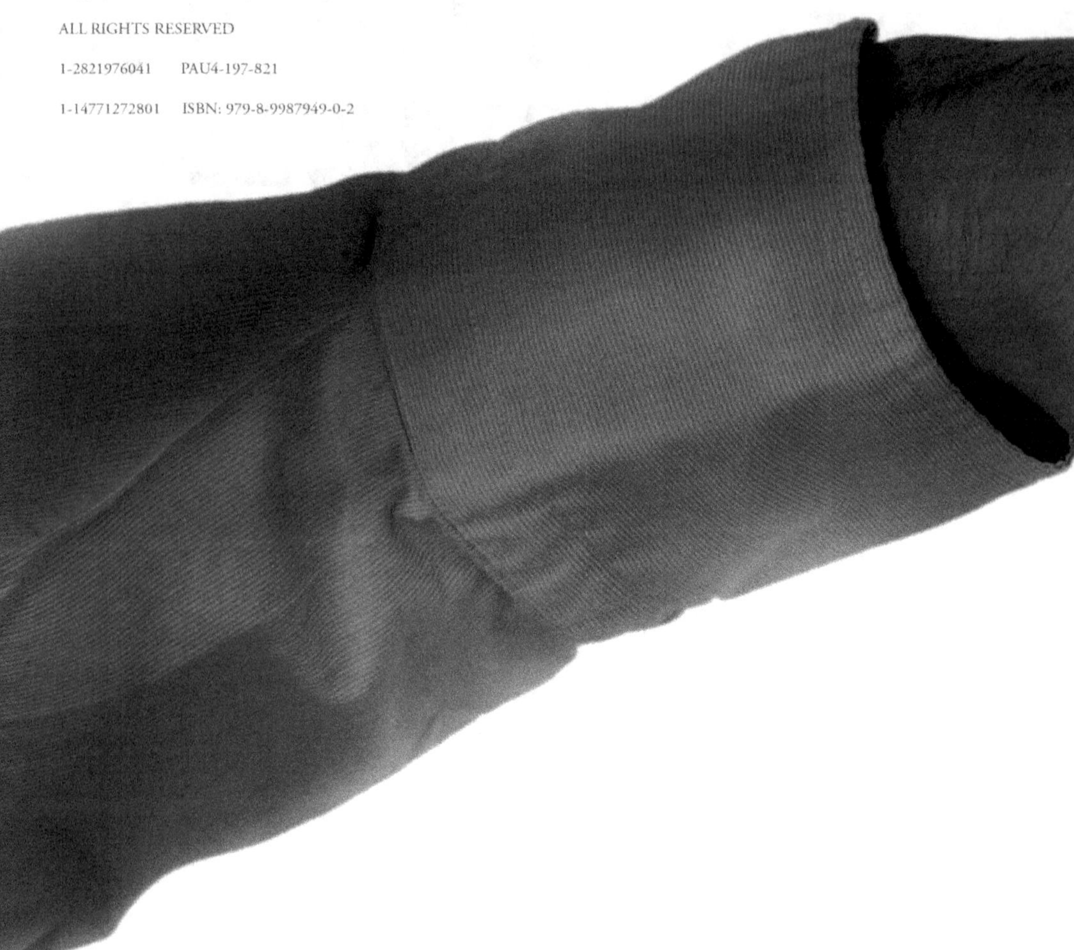

This is a work of fiction. All incidents and dialogue, and all characters with the exception of well-known historical and public figures, are the products of the author's imagination and are not to be construed as real. Any resemblance to persons living or dead is entirely coincidental.

An original publication of Kinda Vague Publishing

For more information email kindavaguepublishing@gmail.com.

First Printing May 2026

10 9 8 7 6 5 4
1-15005324791

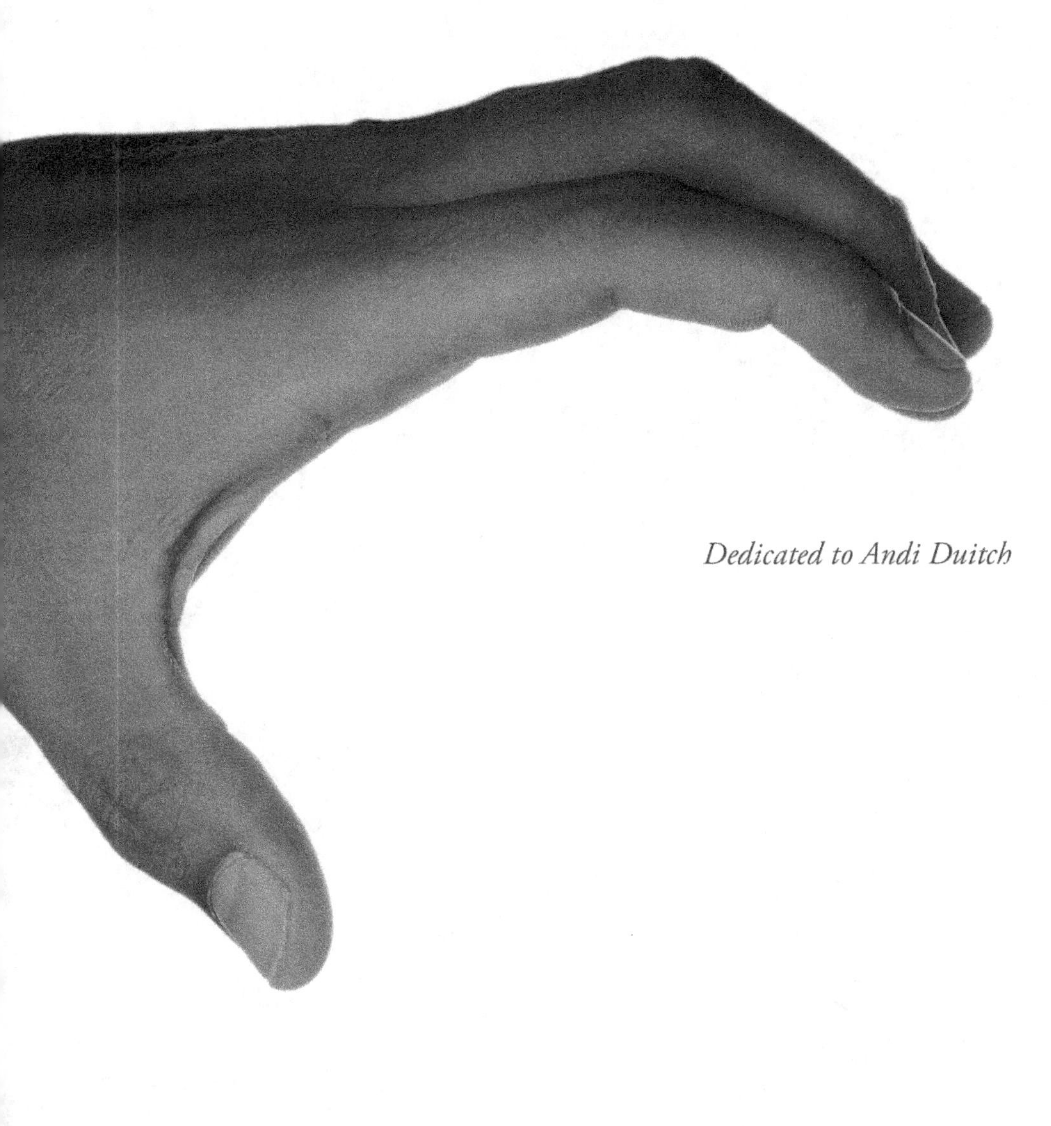

Dedicated to Andi Duitch

TABLE OF CONTENTS

TEN STAGES OF LOVE 8

MALVO HILL 42

GHOST OF
UNION STATION 84

THE TRAGEDY AT
MARSDON MANOR 94

10 STAGES of LOVE
temporary services
ROSE
SECURITY

TEN STAGES OF LOVE

CAST OF CHARACTERS

SHELLY *26 years old, a mermaid with a broken tail*

ROCCO *32 years old, a sailor lost at sea*

CUPID *44 years old, the winged god of love*

PLACE

A rock island, in the middle of the ocean

TIME

Back in the past

SCENE 1

SHELLY *sunbathes on a rock. The waves lap and a seagull calls. We hear the rustling of wings. Then* CUPID *enters, unnoticed*

CUPID: Silence, mortals! I am Cupid. Roman God of desire. And these are the Ten Stages of Love. I'm a demented little cherub. I like pairing mermaids and sailors. I love watching them mate. (SHELLY *sings a dramatic aria)* Allright, now we can begin. *(Offstage, a naval ship crashes into the rock island. The lights flicker red. We hear massive explosions and sailors drowning.* ROCCO *enters, half-submerged, floating on a chest*) Come on, let's look in on them. Shelly and Rocco. He — a ship-wrecked sailor. She — a mermaid with a broken tail. They meet on a rock island, in the wild Atlantic. I see them, but they don't see me. I'm not present. I'm invisible. Inaudible. *(Prances around)* Mermaids are a fascinating part of nature. *(A baby sea turtle crawls by.* SHELLY *picks him up and kisses his bald head)* Some deny their very existence, but mermaids are real. Answer their call and you'll find one. A total Sea-Betty. Part woman, part fish. All wiggle.

SHELLY: All by myself. No one to talk to. It's just me and my misshapen tail. *(Blows a conch shell)*

CUPID: You see, Shelly can't swim because of her injury.

SHELLY: *(Admires herself in a hand mirror)* At least I'm having a good hair day. I don't know what I did differently. Hm. Sometimes it's just effortless. *(Lifts up her eyes and stares at the Sun)* I love the Sun, but I can't get away from it. Red rays. Always in my face. Singeing me. Soothing me. The Sun. Yes, the Sun appears perfectly round, a huge letter O, but it's an optical illusion. A circle is the only shape that can't fall in on itself. Yet stars do all the time. They die and collapse.

CUPID: *(Aims his arrow at* SHELLY) Ahhh. Boy meets girl. *(Shoots* SHELLY) Pheromones are in the air-air-air! *(Shoots* ROCCO) Struck by my arrows, they see each other and are interested. (SHELLY *and* ROCCO *look closely at each other and blush)* When I look at Shelly and Rocco, my heart-strings go— *(We hear a harp play.* SHELLY *and* ROCCO *freeze in place)* Please sit and admire my tableau vivant. A living picture of love. *(Frames them with his fingers)* Stage One: First Blush. *(The lights blink)*

SCENE 2

CUPID: Stage Two: He Overreaches.

ROCCO: Holy mackerel! Your song was mesmerizing. What do you call that?

SHELLY: Scales.

ROCCO: Scales, huh? Did you sing it with me in mind?

SHELLY: No. We just met. I don't even know your name.

ROCCO: Strange. I know your face from somewhere. Hi, I'm Rocco.

SHELLY: *(Flirtingly)* Hi, Rocco.

ROCCO: What's your name?

SHELLY: Shelly.

ROCCO: Oh, you look exotic, Shelly. (*Whistles*) Rare.

SHELLY: What are you doing here?

ROCCO: You know, just lounging.

SHELLY: "Just lounging?" Out on the ocean?

ROCCO: Well, my ship sank and took all hands with it. I'm the sole survivor. See all the smoke? Look. (*Floats over to* SHELLY) Wow! Are you a mermaid?

SHELLY: *(Sarcastically)* No, I'm a goldfish. (*Flaps her tail and smacks her lips*)

ROCCO: *(Smirks)* Hey, mind if I join you? (*Looks her up and down*)

SHELLY: What, you want to come up here?

ROCCO: I want to be where you are.

SHELLY: Please, I have alot of things to do. I can't be bothered.

ROCCO: Oh, you got shit to do? Busy, huh?

SHELLY: Yes. Now please stop talking to me.

ROCCO: Wow, I never met a real Siren before.

SHELLY: Sirens are half-bird.

ROCCO: Oh right, and you got a fish's tail. *(Enamored by her tail)* I can't take my eyes off it. Green-blue scales. Orangey foil. It's reflective.

SHELLY: It's whatever. *(Bats* ROCCO'S *hand away)*
ROCCO: Are you good luck or bad luck?
SHELLY: I'm terrible luck. I don't like you and I don't like your Navy ways.
ROCCO: What? You got other options? *(Pulls on* SHELLY'S *arm, as he climbs up the rocks)* I hooked one. A mermaid. Fuck yeah! (SHELLY *and* ROCCO *freeze. We hear the harp play)*
CUPID: *(Sings)* A GOOD SAILOR'S HARD TO FIND. MERMAIDS ALWAYS GET THE OTHER KIND. BA-BA-BA-BAH. SOME SAY I'M STUPID BUT CUPID'S SMART. BA-BA-BA-BAH. I KNOW THE WORKINGS OF YOUR HEART. BA-BA-BA-BAH. I'M A TRAINED DEAD-EYE WITH MY DARTS. DO-DO-DO-DOH. THEY'RE THROWN AT VITAL BODY PARTS. DO-DO-DO-DOH! SHE GETS PLEASURE FROM CUPID'S FEATHERS. TICKLING HER FLOWERY NETHERS. DO-DO-DO-DOH! *(Frames them with his fingers. The lights blink)*

SCENE 3

CUPID: Stage Three: She Bristles.

SHELLY: Ohhh, that's a big smile you're wearing, sailor.

ROCCO: Well, I smile when I'm happy, I sleep when I'm tired, and I stuff my mouth when I'm hungry. That's just how I am. *(The hatchling crawls by)* Hi!

SHELLY: Hello.

ROCCO: Hey, what's to eat around here, huh? *(Yanks her tail)* How about a light dinner?

SHELLY: Ouch! Rocco! That hurt! Without meaning to, you bruised my tail.

ROCCO: I didn't bruise you. Where?

SHELLY: Right here. I'm not making it up.

ROCCO: Jesus. What are you, made out of tissue paper? Look, I got rough hands, allright? I'm a warfighter.

SHELLY: Well, watch it.

ROCCO: Come on, baby. All your troubles are over, now that I'm around. *(Looks into* SHELLY'S *small mirror, admiring himself)* I'm a well-made man. Tallest officer in the Navy. And the most devastating. *(Rubs* SHELLY'S *tail)* That's right, you can't do better than Old Rocco here.

SHELLY: Don't touch me. *(Slaps* ROCCO *in the face with her tail — his white cap pops off.* SHELLY *and* ROCCO *freeze)*

CUPID: Shelly's no Disneyfied mermaid. That's kid's stuff. Lame! I'm giving Ariel a makeover. I don't like her sweet and vapid. I like her twisted and mean. The bitterer, the betterer. You know? *(Frames* SHELLY *and* ROCCO *with his fingers. The lights blink)*

SCENE 4

ROCCO, *looking into* SHELLY'S *small mirror, shaves with a straight razor.* CUPID *places the baby sea turtle into* SHELLY'S *hands*

CUPID: Stage Four: They Get to Know Each Other.
ROCCO: *(Puts his arm around* SHELLY) Come here. You know I like you, right?
SHELLY: Well, I don't know why.
ROCCO: I do. I just do.
SHELLY: Even though I'm a saltwater bitch? (CUPID *leans on the rock, in profile)*
ROCCO: Who called you that? "A saltwater bitch."
SHELLY: Sailor boy named Scruffy. He said my eyes were dull and fishy. He said that.
ROCCO: That's no way to treat a mermaid. Any mermaid. Tell me, what'd Scruffy do to you?
SHELLY: He whistled at me.
ROCCO: He whistled at you? That's all?
SHELLY: Well, he slapped me around a little too.
ROCCO: Oh yeah? Really?
SHELLY: My father caught us together, over the summer. He took Scruffy down in the coral and drowned him. Then he broke my tailbone. My tail, Rocco. My tail. He snapped it in half. Daddy disabled me.
ROCCO: Uhh, is Daddy coming back, or?
SHELLY: My sister — she's a boat-whore. You can tell a boat-whore by her flirtatious dancing and the seagrass in her hair. My sister wanted to have her way with Scruffy, but I enticed him more.
ROCCO: Well, yeah. He wanted to fuck you.
SHELLY: I'm her baby sister. I shouldn't stand in her way. I can't get engaged,

because she hasn't gotten engaged. The King commands it. My father, the Old Sea King. I'm supposed to produce eggs and diet. That's my only function. Daddy says so all the time.

ROCCO: Uh-huh. And what's your sister like?

SHELLY: She's a vain bitch. Loves attention. Fucking hates me. So big sis told the world. Opened her fat mouth. About me and Scruffy. She said I poisoned him. No, Daddy drowned him. Anyway, her body count is way higher than mine.

ROCCO: Yeah? Tell me about your undersea family. I'd love to learn more.

SHELLY: Well, the Old Sea King disowned me.

ROCCO: Prick.

SHELLY: You're all pricks, Rocco. Please don't get mad.

ROCCO: *(Agitated)* I'm not mad.

SHELLY: Your eyes are turning black.

ROCCO: I'm not. If I wanted to hurt you, I could. But I never would.

SHELLY: Well, we're both susceptible to pain.

ROCCO: Shelly, don't be that way. I've sailed around the world and I've never seen a girl like you. That hair! That smile! Those eyes! That mermaid! You! With the tits! I want you. Your curves craze my brain. Get me all confuzzled.

SHELLY: I'm glad you like me. I want to look good for you.

ROCCO: Shelly, baby. Don't wriggle away. You know how much I love you.

SHELLY: How much?

ROCCO: More than all the stars in the sky.

SHELLY: So you only love me at nighttime, then?

ROCCO: No, all the time. You and your sweet round ass.

SHELLY: You sound like Scruffy.

ROCCO: How many Scruffys have you dated?

SHELLY: Nineteen. (ROCCO *whistles)* You make twenty, big boy.

ROCCO: I'm twentieth?

SHELLY: And counting.

ROCCO: Well, Shelly, I'm wild about you. Obsessed. I'm always wondering, "What's Shelly doing? What's Shelly thinking? What is she going to say next?" (CUPID *hangs on their every word)*

SHELLY: You said you're a warfighter? That you have rough hands?

ROCCO: *(Looks at his hands)* Dirty.

SHELLY: Can you fix me? My crooked tail?

ROCCO: Negative, I can't fix your tail. *(Takes her hand)* No Navyman could. *(Takes off his jumper)* But I can repair a broken heart. *(Touches the crook in* SHELLY'S *tail)* Very easily. (SHELLY *and* ROCCO *freeze*)

CUPID: Oooooh! A tattoo of a mermaid on his shoulder. Looks just like Shelly. Beautiful, but broken. Rocco got her the day he joined the Navy. *(Laughs)* Two fates, twisted together, doomed from the start. *(Laughs more)* Take it from me, a god! *(Frames* SHELLY *and* ROCCO *with his fingers. The lights blink)*

SCENE 5

CUPID: Stage Five: He Gives Her a Gift. (ROCCO *yawns)*

SHELLY: Are you tired?

ROCCO: Yeah, Shelly, I'm tired. My bed is a pile of pointy rocks. I miss my pillow. I miss squeezing dreams out of it. I can't sleep without my pillow. So don't ever ask me that question again, "Are you tired?" Because the answer will always be yes, I'm tired, ok?

SHELLY: Ok, go back to sleep.

ROCCO: I can't sleep. I keep telling you that. *(Snaps his fingers)* Allright, you owe me big time.

SHELLY: Owe you what?

ROCCO: A rubbing. I checked the books. You're overdue. Now pay up. Rub me.

SHELLY: Rocco, please.

ROCCO: Rub me, woman.

SHELLY: You never rub me.

ROCCO: Yes, I do!

SHELLY: Your rubbings are rubbish. *(Scratches him reluctantly)*

ROCCO: Oh yeah, hit that one spot, will you? Oh-ohh-oh. Right there. Oh, that feels delicious. Hey, come on, why aren't you rubbing me? *(Intensely)* Mmmm. More. Don't stop. You're neglecting me, Shelly.

SHELLY: All I do is rub you! Every day, all day.

ROCCO: Do me right, do me wrong, just do me! Do me, do me, do me!

SHELLY: You sailors — you're all the same.

ROCCO: *(Growls)* Quiet, woman. That's enough out of you. *(Regains his composure)* I don't like my merladies talking too much. *(Gently pulls her hair)*

SHELLY: Ouch. Don't touch my hair. *(Brushes her hair)* Uhh! You'll frizz it up. Where's Fitz?

ROCCO: Who?

SHELLY: Fitz. *(The baby turtle passes in front of her)*

ROCCO: Little nut scratch. What's he looking at?

SHELLY: Nothing. See? Nothing. *(Waves at the turtle)* Baby turtles have poor eyesight. That's why they follow the first thing they see after they hatch. It's true. *(Moves — the turtle follows her)* Oh, he's sweet, huh? Look at him. He makes my bosom burst with adoration.

ROCCO: There's no room. He's got to go.

SHELLY: There's always room in my heart for him. Fitz sits in the front row.

ROCCO: Nah.

SHELLY: No one could ever get mad at him. Did you know sea turtles get entangled in the fishing nets? They can't surface for air and drown. But not Fitz. Not my hatchling. He'll perpetuate his species.

ROCCO: Not a chance. *(The hatchling hides)*

SHELLY: Aw, he left us. He'll be back.

ROCCO: *(Dangles a shell necklace)* I got a present for you.

SHELLY: A present?

ROCCO: Mm-hmm.

SHELLY: What is it?

ROCCO: It's a shell necklace.

SHELLY: Oh!

ROCCO: Yeah, I spent the whole morning shelling. Today's our one month anniversary. I wanted to get you champagne and oysters, but, you know.

SHELLY: I drink champagne.

ROCCO: Ok! An oceanful of champagne. I promise only the finest quality. And I always hold true to my promises.

SHELLY: Oh, I love you, I love you, I love you. Oh, you're so good to me, Rocco.

ROCCO: Anything for you, my queen. *(Bows)*

SHELLY: Thank you.

ROCCO: No, thank you, Shelly. Thank you for your kindness. I was a

stranger and you took me in. You shared your home with me. And I'll never forget that. *(Ties the necklace on* SHELLY *from behind, then nibbles on her ear)*
SHELLY: Oh, Rocco. (SHELLY *and* ROCCO *freeze)*
CUPID: A charming liar. He only tells her what she wants to hear. Oh! I've arranged the meetings of a million Shelly and Roccos. A million Rocco and Shellys. I take perverse pleasure in it. Oh, I really fucking do. *(Frames* SHELLY *and* ROCCO *with his fingers. The lights blink)*

SCENE 6

CUPID: Stage Six: Blissful Haaaaaaarmony.

ROCCO: An hour goes by. A week. A month. Time drags on. I'm trapped here! Help! My body needs food. Sustenance. *(Stares at the ocean)* I'm marooned. I can't escape. And I never want to leave. Why would I? I got my seamaid, and that's enough. *(Sweetly)* I'll take you, Shelly. You're a good catch.

SHELLY: Sing me a song, Rocco. A sea chantey.

ROCCO: *(Snaps his fingers and sings)* OH, WHERE DO I BEGIN? LET'S START WITH SOME GIN. THEN RED STRIPE MIGHT PROVE YOUR TYPE. UNTIL THE NEXT BOTTLE OF SIN. I LOVE YELLOW-HEADS. I HAD ONE ONCE. A HOTTIE WITH A BODY, CHARM AND INTELLIGENCE. SHE GAVE ME A CHILD. LIGHT OLIVE COLOR. FIRST IN ORDER OF BIRTH. I MADE MANY MOTHERS. NOBODY'S GOT A KILLER BODY LIKE MY SOMEBODY. LIKE MY LITLLE ODDLING. NOW SHAKE IT NAKED. ALLRIGHT!

SHELLY: Did you call me an oddling?

ROCCO: Shhh. Don't ask questions.

SHELLY: Why not?

ROCCO: Look at those eyebrows. They're so inquisitive. Like two little question marks.

SHELLY: Is that all I have going for me? My eyebrows?

ROCCO: Not just your brows. *(Slides over to her)* Come on now, Shelly Baby. You're driving me mad.

SHELLY: How so?

ROCCO: You got an hourglass figure, and, well, I want to see what time it is.

SHELLY: *(Pulls* ROCCO *close)* Kiss me then, sailor. *(Kisses* ROCCO. SHELLY *and* ROCCO *freeze)*

CUPID: Ah-hah! A perfectly-timed kiss. I drew my bow and sent the arrow to its target. I aimed for the kill. *(Frames* SHELLY *and* ROCCO *with his fingers. The lights blink)*

SCENE 7

CUPID: Stage Seven: A Deeper Connection.

ROCCO: Is dinner ready yet? I'm starving.

SHELLY: *(Tosses salad in a bowl)* Just two seconds. It's almost ripe.

ROCCO: You made sponge? Aw, I hate sponge.

SHELLY: *(Serves* ROCCO) It's your favorite.

ROCCO: Back in the Navy, I ate sardines for every meal, you know. And I smoked a pipe and I never complained. That's how I lived.

SHELLY: Great.

ROCCO: Fuck this. I'm going fishing.

SHELLY: "Going fishing?"

ROCCO: Yeah, you heard me. I'm a pesco.

SHELLY: Did you say pesco? Pesco?

ROCCO: That's right.

SHELLY: Rocco, that is a bogus form of vegetarianism. Killing is killing. Meat is meat. Is that how you view me? *(Flaps her tail)* As bait?

ROCCO: You really want to know?

SHELLY: I asked, didn't I? It's time we had that talk, Rocco.

ROCCO: Later.

SHELLY: No, talk to me now, Rocco.

ROCCO: I don't want to talk. I want to eat. Now serve me some real fucking food.

SHELLY: This is "some real fucking food." Sea vegetables. Here! *(Throws salad at* ROCCO) God! That's the last time I cook for you!

ROCCO: How about turtle soup? It's a great delicacy. Ever try it?

SHELLY: Turtle soup? No, Rocco, I think with my brain, not with my stomach.

ROCCO: Turtle soup! It's easy as one-two-three. One: you crack the shell. Two: you peel it back and discard. Three: you clean off the meat and organs.

Comes with its own bowl too.

SHELLY: Look, I don't want to argue anymore. Eat something. Well dressed greens.

ROCCO: I'm craving meat and I'll kill to get it. (SHELLY *force-feeds him dried kelp — he makes a face)*

SHELLY: You like it? You like it?

ROCCO: I like it. Every bite.

SHELLY: You promise?

ROCCO: I promise.

SHELLY: Love you.

ROCCO: Love you.

SHELLY: Love—achoo!! Achoo! *(Sniffles)* Oh my God. I think I have a cold coming on.

ROCCO: Probably because of your prissy diet.

SHELLY: Achoo! *(Sneezes on* ROCCO) Achoo! (SHELLY *and* ROCCO *freeze)*

CUPID: Can a sailor live off a sirenian diet? I don't eat earthly food, so I don't know. *(Frames* SHELLY *and* ROCCO *with his fingers. The lights blink)*

SCENE 8

ROCCO *drools in his sleep*

CUPID: *(Holds the baby turtle)* Stage Eight: One Hurts the Other.
SHELLY: Rocco! Rocco! Rocco! Rocco! Rocco! Rocco! Wake up! Where's my hatchling? Rocco! Where's my turtle? I can't find Fitz.
ROCCO: *(Awakes)* Don't. Don't wake me up, screaming my name. "Rocco! Rocco!" All panicky and shit. *(Jabs his finger at* SHELLY*)* You hear me? *(Shakes her)* I'm giving you a direct order.
SHELLY: Fine. Ow! Rocco! You scraped some skin off my arm.
ROCCO: Look at me. Look at me! I'm wasting away over here. Fucking barely breathing. Why can't you figure out dinner, huh?
SHELLY: I don't know.
ROCCO: Why is your cooking so bad?
SHELLY: I don't know.
ROCCO: Why don't you have any answers? These are questions I think about. Like where's lunch? How about a little something to eat?
SHELLY: All you got is me, Rocco. So start treating me right. Or I'll turn on you. Achoo! I've been sneezing for weeks. Achoo! *(Coughs, then clears her throat)* God, this stupid cold has made me more, ugh, miserable and tired than usual. Achoo!
ROCCO: Are you allright?
SHELLY: No! I'm sick. And I hope I make you sick too. *(A seagull calls —* ROCCO *calls back menacingly)* Oh, it's going to be one of those days, huh?
ROCCO: Yeah, gloomy. Survive or die. *(Flashes his straight razor — it gleams)* It's eat or be eaten. *(The seagull calls again.* ROCCO *howls with hunger.* CUPID *puts the turtle on the rock)*
SHELLY: Oh! My baby boy. *(Moves away from* ROCCO *— the hatchling follows her)*

ROCCO: *(Picks up the turtle)* He looks good enough to eat.

SHELLY: Give me my turtle. Give me my turtle. What's the matter with you? You're making him cry.

ROCCO: Yeah, yeah. Don't worry about it.

SHELLY: Careful. Be very careful with him. He's endangered!

ROCCO: And I'm not? *(Slashes the turtle with his razor, then gobbles him up)* Mmmm. *(Licks his lips, as the juices dribble down his chin)* Anything for dessert?

SHELLY: *(Beats* ROCCO) What is wrong with you?! *(Cries)* You're a psychopath! Depraved! Sick! *(Hooks her fingernail inside his lip and drags him)*

ROCCO: Hey!

SHELLY: I hate you! I hate you! I hate you! You motherfucker! (SHELLY *and* ROCCO *freeze)*

CUPID: Wow! That's some wild shit. From the land of what the fuck? *(Frames* SHELLY *and* ROCCO *with his fingers. The lights blink)*

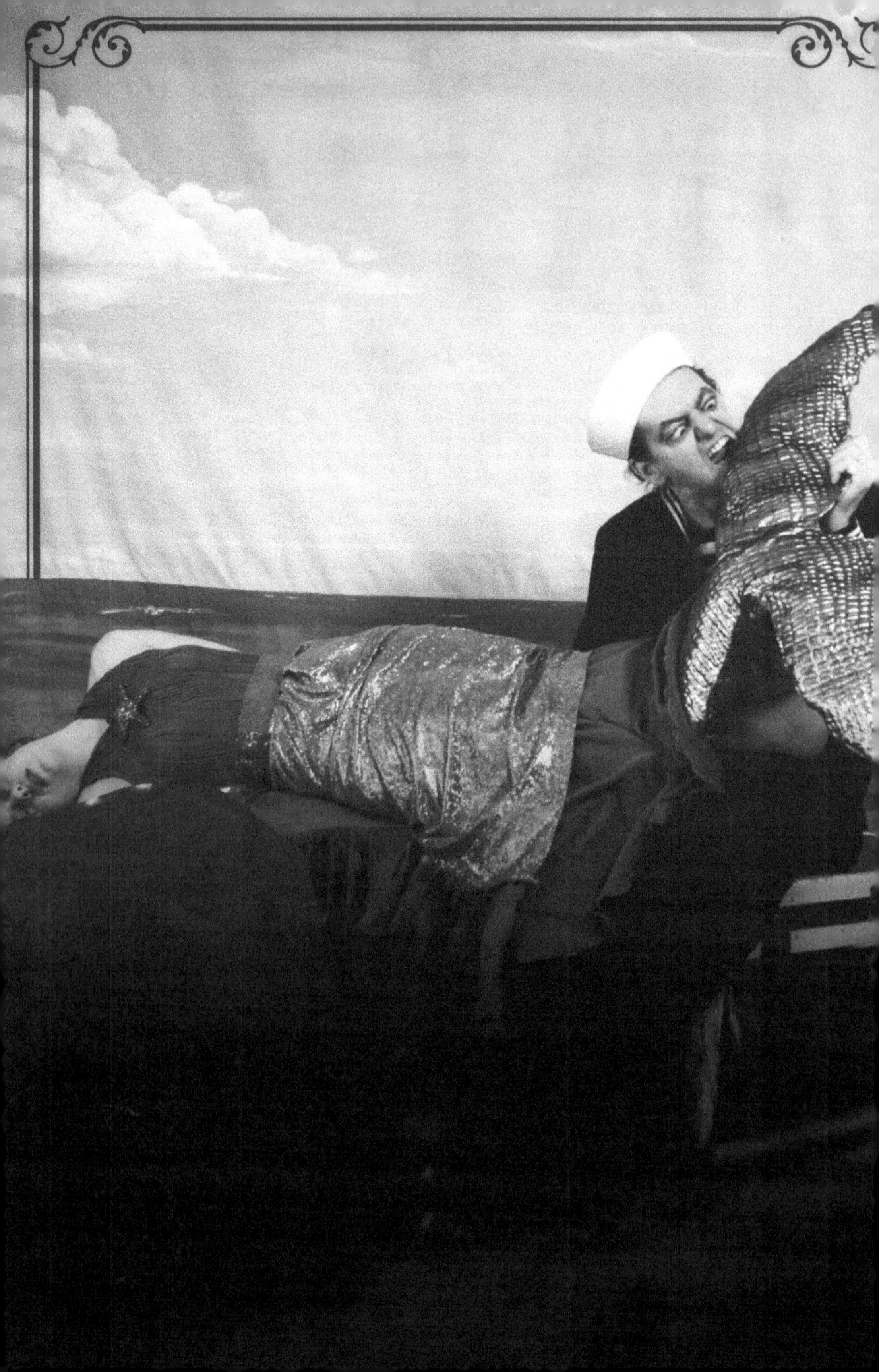

SCENE 9

CUPID: Stage Nine: The Other Gets Revenge.

ROCCO: I'm sorry.

SHELLY: I'll never forgive you, Rocco.

ROCCO: You're just cold. Here, take my jumper. It's fuzzy.

SHELLY: Stay on your side.

ROCCO: Look, Shelly, I'm sorry I appeased my hunger. I'm sorry I wanted to stay alive. I'm sorry you got upset. And I'm sorry it turned into all this.

SHELLY: Oh my God! Stop talking. You're "sorry?" You're just saying words.

ROCCO: Come on, you can't stay mad at Old Rocco.

SHELLY: Look at you. You don't even care.

ROCCO: Allright, I'm sorry for apologizing, then.

SHELLY: Will you shut up and leave me alone? And take your stupid fucking necklace with you! *(Throws her necklace at* ROCCO*)* You killed my hatchling. You came with a knife, you cut him in half and ate him alive.

ROCCO: It's a bad way to die. I admit it. Probably the worst.

SHELLY: *(With contempt)* Don't shut your eyes tonight. I will kill you. I will kill you. I promise, I will kill the one who killed my baby. I will make you pay.

ROCCO: *(Takes out his knife)* Here, take the razor. Take it! Take it! Cut me, come on.

SHELLY: I can't.

ROCCO: *(Pins her down)* You saltwater bitch. Don't look at me that way.

SHELLY: Stop it! Get off me!

ROCCO: You drowned the Navy. You're cold-blooded, Shelly. You killed my friends. They lost their lives. It's appalling.

SHELLY: *(Pleads for her life)* That was before I met you. Before we fell in love.

ROCCO: *(Twists* SHELLY'S *arm)* Don't fight me, don't fight me.

SHELLY: Ow! Your grip is so strong! *(In pain)* Please, I love you, Rocco. I love you. I love everything about you. I just want to be with you, sweetheart.

ROCCO: That means nothing to me. *(Cuts* SHELLY'S *tail with a downward slice — blood and fish guts fly out. The lights flash red —* SHELLY *screams)* Very little blood. *(Red-handed)* Only so much to lose. *(Makes the opening of her wound bigger — she screams louder)* Ah, fine and delicate work. (SHELLY *tries to escape, but he blocks her, standing with his back to the audience)*

SHELLY: *(Flops around)* Oh God! What are you doing to me? *(Panic-stricken)* You fucking carnivore! You filleted me.

ROCCO: Well, a man's got to eat.

SHELLY: *(In shock)* Ha, ha, ha, ha. Ha, ha, ha, ha. Your dinner is getting cold, Rocco. Ha, ha, ha.

ROCCO: What are you laughing at? What's so funny? Huh?

SHELLY: You'll find out. *(Goes limp.* ROCCO *eats her raw.* SHELLY *and* ROCCO *freeze)*

CUPID: This fucking guy here. I mean, what a dildo! I feel sorry for what happened to Shelly. You know, she's a mermaid, she's pretty, she gets gutted. It's nothing personal. "A man's got to eat." *(Frames* SHELLY *and* ROCCO *with his fingers. The lights blink)*

SCENE 10

The rock is stained with blood. SHELLY *floats upside down in the water*

CUPID: Stage Ten: Salmonella Poisoning.

ROCCO: *(Moans)* Oh, my stomach! *(Grips his stomach)* Ohhh. *(Screams in pain)* God, what did I eat, bad bacteria? *(Trips backwards on the rocks and falls)* Please, I'm begging you. *(Vomits behind the rock)* Aarghhhhh. I'm covered in this pink rash. Fucking mermaids — they're toxic. *(Dies of poisoning. We hear* SHELLY *laughing from beyond the beyond.* CUPID *frames* SHELLY *and* ROCCO *with his fingers. The lights blink)*

CUPID: Well, mortals, there you have it. The Ten Stages of Love. Depicted by I, Cupid. Mischievous Matchmaker. Allright, how about it for Shelly and Rocco, huh? *(Claps)* Come on! I hope you enjoyed the different phases. We moved from "First Blush" to "Blissful Harmony" to "One Hurts the Other" until finally "Salmonella Poisoning." Hey, you cannot fault the gods. All he had to do was eat kelp and he'd be alive today, and in love. *(We hear the harp play)* Why didn't she whip him with her tail? Only I know why. *(We hear the harp again)* The mermaid and the sailor. *(Flitters his wings)* One always consumes the other. *(Flies away. The Sun fades. The stage darkens)*

End of Play

temporary services

MALVO HILL

CAST OF CHARACTERS

MALVO HILL *19-40 years old*

MALVO HILL JUNIOR *6 years old*

TEENAGE MALVO *16 years old*

TONY SAVINO *36 years old*

OFFICER KLUNT *37 years old*

OPRAH WINFREY *35 years old*

GARCIA *16 years old*

DAD *41 years old*

MAYOR *40 years old*

ANNOUNCER

PLACE

Denver, Colorado

TIME

1995 — Present-day

SCENE 1

MALVO HILL JUNIOR, *a rat, under a spotlight. He speaks to the audience, pacing nervously*

MALVO HILL JUNIOR: *(In a New York accent)* Hey oho! Oh! This is my rathole. I see ya. I see ya peeping through the opening. You're asking for trouble, ya see. I'm from New York City and I'll bust your brains out. Nah, I ain't scared of nothin'. Not this stinky-fink. What, do I look like a burrata-lover to you? Lemme tell ya something, the softer the cheese, the fatter the rat. Yeah, not me, man. I'm 'core. I eat everything. Mace, shrapnel, batteries. There's an unlimited supply of human trash. All you can gnaw. Yeah, that's right! I'm a big, mean, fire-breathing subway rat. Straight out the sewer pipe. So shut up! Don't talk to me. I'm not in the mood. I heard about boot parties. Crush fetishes. Oh, you find that funny, huh? Come on, make a move. I'll fight ya. I'll fight ya to the finish. Oh, you wanna play a game? Allright. Allright, let's play a game, then. If I win, I'll crawl up your body and nibble on your nose. Oh, and if you win, uh, I'll give you my left claw. The hind one. As a good-luck charm. Allright? Hey, be careful. If you corner me, I'll jump at ya. Jump straight at ya. Ok? Hey, what are you doing? I scratch. Hey! I bite. *(Bares his teeth)* Stop it. Go on, get off. *(Pause)* Grabbin' me... *(Drops the accent and bravado)* Ok. Ok. You got me. You got me. I'm not actually from New York City. Just talkin' tough. I'm really just a common house rat. Truth of the matter is, the city — it intimidates me. My friends get killed there. Plump rats. Too fat to run. Terriers — they snatch us up in their jaws. *(We hear a small dog bark)* That bark! Terriers. Terriers! Set loose by crazy people. Who can't handle their personal lives, so they kick us. Flatten us. I live in constant fear of being stepped on. Of impending doom. When I look up, I see the bottom of a shoe. Stomp, stomp, tromp. I'm shoe-panicked. And you're sitting there aloof. Aloof! All humans are. But look, I don't wanna get into it with you.

Some of you are nice. Take my late master, for instance. Malvo was a saint. I'm Malvo Hill Junior. I was named after him. Malvo died at forty. So young, so sad. A chandelier dropped on his head at the Brown Palace Hotel. I heard the chandelier that fell on Malvo was haunted. A vengeful ornamental entity. That's what they said. All I know is, Malvo raised an assortment of animals. but he spent the most time with me. His favorite playmate. I followed him around the house wherever he went. He used to dress me up like a young prince. Glowing white tuxedo, black top hat, lil' bowtie. We drank champagne and ate caviar. Oh, I was the classiest rat in Denver.

MALVO: *(Voice-over)* Introducing my new bambino! Malvo Hill Junior. He first opened his beady little eyes on July 25th, 2017, measuring four inches long. I'm bundling Malvo Hill Junior off to rosy Wash Park. He's my son. I'm proud of my rat baby.

MALVO HILL JUNIOR: You know, Malvo didn't have any children, so I'm the only one who can carry on his family name. Seriously. His bloodline ends with me: Malvo Hill Junior. It's only right I tell Malvo's story. Malvo AKA Float Bloy. This one is about his first experience of love. Watch "Float Boy's Confession."

SCENE 2

A stone-gray police interrogation room. MALVO *sits in a red chair behind a table. He wears a tropical shirt, a pair of slippers and a tall, greased-back pompadour. Ringed around his belly is an inflatable pool floaty.* OFFICER KLUNT, *uniformed, enters the interrogation room and proceeds to pat down* MALVO. *Perched high on the wall is a TV, playing footage of a fashion show at low volume*

OFFICER KLUNT: *(Throws a file down on the table)* Float Boy, huh? *(*MALVO *laughs)* What's your name, Float Boy?
MALVO: You just said it.
OFFICER KLUNT: "Float Boy?" That's on your birth certificate? "Float Boy?"
MALVO: Yeah.
OFFICER KLUNT: You got anything sharp on you?
MALVO: Only my intellect.
OFFICER KLUNT: Ha, ha. You think you're pretty funny, huh?
MALVO: Oh, you know it, baby!
OFFICER KLUNT: You wanna take a lie detector test?
MALVO: Hook me up. No problem.
OFFICER KLUNT: You're a sick fuck, aren't you?
MALVO: No, I'm a nice, sweet boy.
OFFICER KLUNT: I don't believe that for a minute.
MALVO: I'll admit it, Officer Klunt. I'm missing some basic human features like shame, you know?
OFFICER KLUNT: Humping your lil' floaty. I get it. No! It's wrong!
MALVO: But it feels right. *(Spins the floaty around his midsection)* You got questions for me. What, man, what?
OFFICER KLUNT: Yeah! I got questions. I'm going to nail you. *(Brandishes*

his baton)

MALVO: Oh, ok. With that baton? 'Cause I don't have that fetish, like you. I don't stick it up my ass.

OFFICER KLUNT: I don't enjoy shit getting stuck in my ass.

MALVO: If you don't enjoy it, then why do you do it? Tell me. I'm curious. What kinda stuff do you put up there? *(*OFFICER KLUNT *beats the floaty with his baton)* No more, no more. No, please, no. Ooh, ooh. Ahhh! More! *(Laughs like a hyena)*

OFFICER KLUNT: You like that shit?

MALVO: Yeah.

OFFICER KLUNT: You're gonna enjoy your home for the next four to twelve years. Yeah, we're gonna keep you, 'cause we know… that you have some affiliations…

MALVO: What? I'm me. I'm Float Boy. I operate alone.

OFFICER KLUNT: Yeah, everybody knows about Float Boy.

MALVO: Uh-huh… Whatever you say, man, that's what I am.

OFFICER KLUNT: This is the file on Float Boy. Years of stacking up floaties and popping 'em.

MALVO: Ha, ha!!

OFFICER KLUNT: Is this the kinda man you wanna be remembered as?

MALVO: Float boy, not man, jerkoff. Get it right, huh? Do your research. Float Boy!

OFFICER KLUNT: Yeah, I don't understand where you went wrong.

MALVO: Ha, ha!!

OFFICER KLUNT: Mama didn't love you much? Daddy loved you too much?

MALVO: Lemme start at the beginning. It all happened when I was thirteen, at the pool, ok? I got an erection. The girls laughed. I ran away and I fell dick-first on my lil' floaty. After that, my pink floaty has been my main squeeze. She never refuses me sex. I love her.

OFFICER KLUNT: If you wanna do it in your bathtub, fine. Fuck away. Have a good time. Do it in public, you're a pervert. That's a disorder. *(Flips through the files)*
MALVO: That's my fetish. I have to be outside, under the Sun, in the raw. Exposed. That's my fetish, man! You caught me. I'll give you credit. You caught me on that wobbly highway sign. Making good loving to my floatable. You know, I like to hook up with my baby in public. So I'm doing my thing. Huh, uh, uh! I got a good rhythm going. Then I look down and see your patrol car, right underneath me. I think, "*Oh fuck!*" I go down the ladder, scale the highway wall, into my little apartment. But you got me.
OFFICER KLUNT: 'Cause I know how to do my job.
MALVO: Here's my confession. Write this shit down. I'm ready to confess.
OFFICER KLUNT: What's your name? *(Starts writing)*
MALVO: My name is Float Boy. I love to hear it squeak. Squeak, squeak, squeak. It's a love affair, ok? She makes my heart throb. And my... well, you know. But I can't give pleasure to inanimate objects. I know that.
OFFICER KLUNT: Right. You can't get off like that.
MALVO: Who are you to tell me I can't get off with my girlfriend?
OFFICER KLUNT: She's not your girlfriend. She's a toy. Go look in my closet, you'll see blowup dolls. Those are real plastic. This is weird. When you're having sex with a blowup doll, it means something, 'cause they got legs and arms and eyes.
MALVO: Man, you dunno what's between me and my floaty. You just dunno. I'm talking. Lemme talk! This is my confession. Ha, ha! Yeah, I know I'm not perfect. Are you perfect? You come to work intoxicated.
OFFICER KLUNT: I'm a cop.
MALVO: You're a lamedick.
OFFICER KLUNT: I'm gonna be detective in no time 'cause of you.
MALVO: Look, I have an irresistible impulse, allright? I can't help it, ok? Help me! Help me! 'Cause I can't help myself.

OFFICER KLUNT: Oh, I'm gonna help you. *(Squirms around in his chair)*
MALVO: What are you looking for? *(*OFFICER KLUNT *squirms more)* What are you sitting on? You uncomfortable? *(Indicating his baton)* Is that the broomstick that made you a woman? What's going on?
OFFICER KLUNT: I'm trying to think how I wanna handle you.
MALVO: I heard you're into batons. And anal beads. You like to reuse 'em.
OFFICER KLUNT: This is how it's gonna play out. You're gonna go to jail tonight.
MALVO: Is that before or after you grudge-fuck me with a plunger?
OFFICER KLUNT: That's gonna happen later.
MALVO: Ok, I'm ready.
OFFICER KLUNT: After you go to bed.
MALVO: Ok. Just wake me up. I wanna be surprised.
OFFICER KLUNT: You're gonna be surprised. 'Cause I'm gonna be inside you deep, boy.
MALVO: Allright. Don't tell me when, just do it.
OFFICER KLUNT: I'm gonna need your floaty. *(Closes the file on Float Boy)*
MALVO: Take your glasses off. I wanna look at your eyes. Are they pinned back? What are you on, man? Your eyes look demonic, they're so red.
OFFICER KLUNT: I guarantee you what.
MALVO: What?
OFFICER KLUNT: I'm taking you down, son.
MALVO: Don't say that. Come on, be cool. We're both into weird sex. Tell me 'bout your torn anus.
OFFICER KLUNT: Well, first I like to be slapped...
MALVO: What about your baton? You don't stick that up your ass?
OFFICER KLUNT: Nah-uh.
MALVO: Uh-huh, uh-huh. I've heard 'bout you, Officer Klunt. How much room do you have up there? You got your buttplug in right now?
OFFICER KLUNT: At least I don't fuck plastic floaties. That's not part of my

nature. My mama told me better than that.

MALVO: Well, you know, that's the difference between me and you. *(Turns his chair around and faces the TV)* Hey, do me a favor, change the channel.

OFFICER KLUNT: Excuse me?

MALVO: I said change the channel. Hurry up.

OFFICER KLUNT: Shut your face! Or I'll smack you so hard it clears your complexion.

MALVO: Klunt, just take it easy, allright?

OFFICER KLUNT: Fuckin' goofball, you. *(The TV plays footage of a cooking contest)*

MALVO: I left a box of donuts for you, for all the screws, behind the counter.

OFFICER KLUNT: A box a donuts, huh?

MALVO: Uh-huh. And at the bottom of the box was a Polaroid of all the donuts lined up on my dick.

OFFICER KLUNT: Really?

MALVO: I was just trying to romanticize the counter lady. You know the counter lady. The one with the big elbows. "Don't touch the counter! Don't cross the yellow line!"

OFFICER KLUNT: Well, did you touch the counter? Because you were certainly warned.

MALVO: I don't listen to people who yell at me. (*We hear the TV get louder.* MALVO *stands up and runs across the room, then headbutts the TV. He smashes his face and falls down. The TV flickers)*

OFFICER KLUNT: Oh, for fuck's sake. *(*MALVO *recovers. He extends his hand to* OFFICER KLUNT, *who slaps it away)*

MALVO: I give you my hand in friendship and... what do you do? You slap it away.

OFFICER KLUNT: You're arrogant! Everything about you is arrogant! Even your haircut is arrogant.

MALVO: Yeah, and?

OFFICER KLUNT: And the TV stays on. "Food Planet." That's my favorite program.

MALVO: "Food Planet?" I'm starving. It makes me wanna lick the screen. You know Oprah's on. Oprah Winfrey. She's live right now. Oprah's all about the hugs. Not light hugs, but deep embraces. Once I saw Oprah spread her arms around the camera and squeeze the world! *(The TV plays footage of perp walks)* So what's up? I gotta call a bondsman, or?

OFFICER KLUNT: Yeah. You get rolled, you get bonded, you go free. Like that. Bondsman's fifteen percent, allright? Fifteen percent of your bail. And a hundred bucks for court costs. *(The TV plays footage of the stock market crashing)*

MALVO: Man...

OFFICER KLUNT: Call a friend.

MALVO: What friends.

OFFICER KLUNT: Doesn't matter. You couldn't call 'em anyway. You can only make collect calls from jail. And alotta phones don't accept collect calls. 'Cause there's a fee you gotta pay upfront, which most people don't. So the payphones are blocked.

MALVO: Well, I'm double fucked, I guess. You know, by the court system and the phone company. It's a conspiracy against me. To hold me prisoner. *(The TV plays footage of the Oprah Winfrey show)* Oh, look, look, look… the counter lady! She turned her back. Now's my chance.

OFFICER KLUNT: Take it! *(Cocks his fist)*

MALVO: Ahh! Don't! Stop! Don't stop. Come on, what are you waiting for?

OFFICER KLUNT: Shit.

MALVO: What?

OFFICER KLUNT: Anything you say can and will be used against you in the court of law. If you refuse to talk to me or have an attorney, I will appoint one to you.

MALVO: Ok, I did it. I confess. Put me away.

OFFICER KLUNT: *(Writes on* MALVO'S *file)* "Guilty."

MALVO: Oh God, no… Oh no, oh no. Please don't put me away.

OFFICER KLUNT: Oh no, it's a sex crime. You'll be out in, like, fifteen minutes.

MALVO: Oh cool.

OFFICER KLUNT: Yeah.

MALVO: Thanks, Klunt!

OPRAH: *(On the television)* Now come here, you. Let's get our snuggle on.

*(*OFFICER KLUNT *exits.* MALVO *watches* OPRAH *on the TV, mid-hug. He falls asleep)*

SCENE 3

OPRAH'S *television studio.* OPRAH *stands in front of the audience, holding a big card with her name written on it. The Oprah logo is projected behind her.* MALVO *sits in a chair, center stage, with an inflatable pool floaty around his belly. We hear R&B music*

ANNOUNCER: *(Voice-over)* Oprah's lost episode. Set to air April 14th, 1999. Due to the nature of the topic, executives decided not to release this episode. Opting to sell the interview to The Jerry Springer Show. For the sanity of the viewers, The Jerry Springer Show declined their proposal.
OPRAH: Hi, babies! Welcome back to the show. Today's episode is called "Rubber Lovers." Our first guest is twenty years old. Comes from New York. Ladies and gentlemen, please meet Float Boy.
MALVO: Hey! How you doin', Oprah?
OPRAH: I'm doing well. Thank you for coming, Float Boy.
MALVO: Thank you so much for having me.
OPRAH: Of course.
MALVO: I probably shouldn't tell you this, but…
OPRAH: Oh, please, you can speak openly.
MALVO: Well, I got caught ass-naked in my grandma's swimming pool. Yeah, making love to her lil' pink raft. *(*OPRAH *and the audience gasp. "Float Boy, lonely 20 something year old" is projected behind her)* Oh yes! I was kissing it. I was stroking it. Oh! But, I mean, it's not just sex. She captured my heart, Oprah. I mean it. We have a real relationship. We spend time together. We have all kinds of laughs, you know? But the neighbors reported us. Ok? I understand. They don't wanna see me, getting raw on this floatable. I totally get it. And my grandma? She's got a right to be ashamed.
OPRAH: Yeah.
MALVO: I know, I gotta pull the plug on Float Boy. I'm blowing it! *(The*

audience laughs) I know all that. Ok? So I'm here to apologize publicly to my grandmother. I'm sorry, Grandma. *(The audience applauds)* I'll never violate another floaty again. *("Float Boy promises grandma to never violate floaties again" is projected)* I'm getting my life together. Ok? I just turned twenty years old. I gotta knock this shit off.

OPRAH: Mm-hmm.

MALVO: Right here, right now. But lemme tell ya, Oprah. Everybody needs a little love in their life. And very, very few get it. Each day, we come closer to death, right? So why not have a lil' pervy fun? You know what I'm sayin'? *(Caresses the pool float. The audience boos)* I mean, this floaty is, like, elastic. It's slippery. It's so—

OPRAH: —gross! *(The audience groans)*

MALVO: Well, at least I'm wearing a rubber, right? *(The audience laughs)*

OPRAH: Oh God. Oh, this is too embarrassing to air.

MALVO: Ok, Oprah. Whatever you say.

OPRAH: Float Boy, you chucklehead. Go out and get a girlfriend. Someone sweet and soft and warm. *("Oprah suggests Float Boy date someone like her" is projected)*

MALVO: Look, don't laugh at me, allright? I've never been on TV before.

OPRAH: I'm not laughing at you. The people are laughing. But I would never, no. *(*MALVO *laughs at the audience's hostile jeers. We hear chants of "O-prah! O-prah!")* Ok, many of you have heard about the contest that Float Boy won. The prize? My voice as the greeting on his answering machine!

MALVO: Ha ha!

OPRAH: Yes, a personal message, which I will record now. (*Holds down a button on* MALVO'S *answering machine)* Hello, I'm Oprah Winfrey. Float Boy is away. I'm receiving his calls and taking messages. Truth is, Float Boy thinks you're stupid. He thinks you only have two brain cells and they're both arguing.

MALVO: Heh, heh!

OPRAH: But I think you're sweet. You want a hug? What's wrong with a hug? I've never been turned down for a hug before. I'll embosom you! Because I'm Oprah. America's Childless Mother! I really am, I'm your surrogate hugger. Ooh baby. *(The answering machine beeps)*

MALVO: Ha, ha, ha! Thanks, Oprah. You're such a nice person.

OPRAH: Oh please.

MALVO: Oh yeah. Full of good advice. You're always dispensing wisdom and Oprah-sized hugs to random strangers like me. *(*OPRAH *laughs)* You know, I'm a fruit-pop, but that's ok. No, really. There's something wrong with my brain, you know. My grandpa was the same way. Wacked-out! Grandpa did a thing. Thirty years ago. Not that thing. He did the other thing. No, he did the other other other thing.

OPRAH: Ah, yes.

MALVO: Yeah, he sold unlicensed guns to an off-duty FBI agent. Allright? Off-duty! The fed was an entrapper! Ok? So Jacinto got sent to federal prison on a bum rap. Jacinto, but everybody called him Jack. Jack was a refrigerator door painter, you see. And he drove brand-new Cadillacs. Well, he caught a charge. Criminal sale of firearms. He made one mistake and spent the last thirty years behind walls. Thirty years! Bum fuckin' luck. Destroyed his life. Finally, he's out. He just got released a week ago. Ok? Now he's an ex-con with a second chance. It's 1999 and he's been gone a long time. I'm his grandson, right? I threw him a getting-out-of-jail party. And I baked him a titty cake. Decorated it too. With candles that spelled out "Welcome Home, Grandpa. Let's Do Blow and Get Blown." *(Laughs with* OPRAH*)* What do you think, Oprah? Pretty good? Next to the cake, I had a lil' jar of sugar and a party favor. *(Blows a party favor)* Then I shoved grandpa's face in the titty cake.

OPRAH: Aah!

MALVO: "Feel like a pair of boobs, Grandpa?"

OPRAH: Well, coming up next, a letter from Float Boy's grandmother. Let's read it, shall we?

MALVO: Hoo-hoo!!

OPRAH: *(Reads a handwritten letter out loud)* "Dear Oprah: I'm writing to complain about my husband, Jack."

MALVO: Jacinto.

OPRAH: "We've been married fifty-five years. I've known my husband my whole life. He has always treated me well." Oh, I'm sorry, I get so emotional.

MALVO: Me too.

OPRAH: "But due to unfortunate circumstances, the federal government separated us for thirty years. Jack had no one to hang out with but convicts. While I'm happy he's still attracted to me, Jack's desire for love-making is insatiable."

MALVO: Go, grandpa!

OPRAH: "I mean, I'm a seventy year old grandmother. And my husband is a sexual jaguar! He can't keep his hands off me, or his tongue out of my mouth. He's trying to get thirty years worth of sex in our retirement age."

MALVO: Heh, heh, heh.

OPRAH: "I understand wanting to make up for lost time, but enough is enough. When are we caught up? God, we do it constantly. Every five minutes. It's ridiculous. We literally have sex all morning, all afternoon, all evening." *(The audience gasps)* Oh, this poor old lady.

MALVO: What? I don't understand. What's the problem?

OPRAH: "He's a maniac and I'm exhausted! Anytime I cook or wash the dishes or do the laundry or talk on the phone, he's jumping me. Please help! I'm sorry for the sloppy handwriting. I hope you understand." Yes. *(Shows the audience Grandma Hill's letter, her handwriting squiggled across the page)* "Sincerely, Jackhammered in Jamacia, Queens." *(Looks directly into the camera)*

MALVO: Oh yeah.

OPRAH: Well, folks. That's all we have for you today. Thanks for watching Oprah! *(MALVO laughs wildly, then blows his party favor)* Tune in tomorrow!

Bye, babies! —Float Boy! Thank you so much for being my special guest. *(Offers* MALVO *a hug)*

MALVO: Thanks, Oprah. *(Accepts her hug)* I always wanted to be in the cuddle club. *(We hear R&B music. The Oprah logo is projected)*

OPRAH: Bye, everyone! *(Throws big kisses)* Mwah! Mwah! Mwah!

SCENE 4

MALVO HILL JUNIOR, *under a spotlight*

MALVO HILL JUNIOR: *(To the audience)* A rat! Rats don't deserve to exist, right? Why should a rat have a life? We're the lowest animal in creation, worthless. Nothing compared to a human. "You rat! You son-of-a-snitch rat! Call Vermin-Killers! There's a critter in the house! Crack his skull. He carries disease. He steals. He smells. Drown that hairy intruder!" My name means fourteen different insults and I've heard 'em all. But you know what? You're the hideous monster, not me. Never forget the bubonic plague. How many millions of rodents had to die because of filthy peasants? You blame us for all the problems in the world. Target us. We're always grinded underfoot. Never safe. You people think we're a threat to the neighborhood, but that's you! Humankind. You're brutal by nature, and that's never gonna change. It only gets worse and worse. Well, maybe I shouldn't lump you all together. That's a mistake. My foster dad was cool. Malvo. I was devoted to him. We had a bond. His natural father? NOT NICE. He abused Malvo as a child. Flashback to 1995. Malvo just turned sixteen. He barely made it to seventeen all in one piece. Whole.

SCENE 5

TEENAGE MALVO *lies in bed, staring up at the ceiling.* GARCIA *steps out of the closet*

GARCIA: Good morning, Malvo. How are you feeling?
TEENAGE MALVO: I'm dead inside, that's how I'm feeling.
GARCIA: Nah, you're not dead inside. You just smoke too much pot.
TEENAGE MALVO: I'm telling you, Garcia, I'm empty.
GARCIA: Empty, huh?
TEENAGE MALVO: Empty as the eye of a needle.
GARCIA: I'll tell you what, man, give it like five minutes. You'll feel better. You're very temperamental. You know that, Malvo? I mean, one minute you're sweet, then you're angry, then you're sad. And, you know, sometimes people can fuck right off. *(Moves to the window)*
TEENAGE MALVO: No, don't go, Garcia. You can stay in my closet. Outta the cold and outta the rain.
GARCIA: What are you so fuckin' mopey about, anyway, huh? *(*TEENAGE MALVO *shrugs)* Malvo, are you already high? *(*TEENAGE MALVO *smiles)* Who gave you money?
TEENAGE MALVO: Nobody.
GARCIA: Allright, then who gave you weed?
TEENAGE MALVO: What weed? Have you seen my pipe, Garcia? I lost it.
GARCIA: Isn't that the classic stoner question.
TEENAGE MALVO: Well, did you take it?
GARCIA: Hey, don't look at me. I'm just standing here.
TEENAGE MALVO: You're a thief! That's why your parents kicked you out, isn't it?
GARCIA: Hey, nah. They kicked me out because I never pass my classes. I never get above a "D."

TEENAGE MALVO: Yeah?

GARCIA: Well, yeah. And I shot my dad's revolver off in the backyard. Used my sister's stuffed animal as target practice. Mom called the cops. I ran. She said, "don't come back!"

TEENAGE MALVO: Jesus.

GARCIA: Yeah, look at this. *(Pulls out a gun)* A revolver in my pocket. But no pipe. See?

TEENAGE MALVO: Whoa.

GARCIA: I mean, come on. Take? From you? After all you've done for me? Letting me stay here, when I didn't have anywhere else to go? Letting me sleep under your dad's nose? No way.

TEENAGE MALVO: Well, could you help me look for it?

GARCIA: Malvo. It's in your ass pocket. You've been sitting on it.

TEENAGE MALVO: Shit.

GARCIA: You fuckin' pothead.

TEENAGE MALVO: Look, I'm a pot-smoker, not a pothead. There's a big difference, allright?

GARCIA: Ok, whatever you say, 'head.

TEENAGE MALVO: *(Smokes weed out of a glass pipe)* Hey, hit this, Garcia. *(Coughs, then elbows* GARCIA*)*

GARCIA: Nah. Boring.

TEENAGE MALVO: Fucking boring? This shit is rocket propellant.

GARCIA: *(Elbows* TEENAGE MALVO*)* Hey, uh, Malvo, is your dad up?

TEENAGE MALVO: My dad? *(Hides his pipe)* He never sleeps. I heard him last night, stomping around the whole time. It felt like he was standing on my head.

GARCIA: Well, be on guard. If he comes down here, you need to defend yourself, ok?

TEENAGE MALVO: You dunno my dad. He's got a heavy hand.

GARCIA: Yeah, you might get knocked down, but he'll think twice next time. I fuckin' slapped my pop and guess what?

TEENAGE MALVO: What?

GARCIA: He backed down and left. Yeah, I dislocated his jaw and he never touched me again. I mean, what kinda father wants to fight his son? It's fuckin' ridiculous.

TEENAGE MALVO: What do I say to him?

GARCIA: You say, "You come at me again, you'll pay the price."

TEENAGE MALVO: That doesn't sound like me.

GARCIA: Well, man, just say whatever comes into your head.

TEENAGE MALVO: He's crazy, you know. That new truck he got? Well, first his old one got stolen. But he's actually the one who stole it. He abandoned it in a parking lot, collected the insurance money. And the worst part is I think he blamed me.

GARCIA: He what?

TEENAGE MALVO: Yeah, he blamed me. He blamed me. He's coming. Get back in the closet, Garcia. Hide! *(*GARCIA *hides in the closet.* DAD *enters)*

DAD: Who the fuck are you talking to, huh? Answer me! You got somebody in here?

TEENAGE MALVO: No.

DAD: Don't mouth off, Malvo!

TEENAGE MALVO: All I said was "no."

DAD: Ok, super genius Malvo. All you do is sit around here all day, talkin' dumb shit. How 'bout a lil' tough love? What do you think, huh? *(Raises his fist)*

TEENAGE MALVO: Please, Dad! Please!

DAD: "Please, Dad!" Christ, you're so fuckin' whiny! Are you afraid of me?

TEENAGE MALVO: *(Whimpers)* No.

DAD: Look at me!

TEENAGE MALVO: Please don't slap me!

DAD: "Please don't slap me!" You know what makes me wanna slap you?

When you say, "Please, Dad, don't slap me." *(Slaps* TEENAGE MALVO*)*

TEENAGE MALVO: Ahhhh! *(Cries)*

DAD: "Whoo hoo hoo!"

TEENAGE MALVO: I didn't do anything.

DAD: You never do anything, bum-ass! Why don't you clean your room? Would you do that? Could you fuckin' clean something? For fuck's sake.

TEENAGE MALVO: Please don't slam that! Please don't slam that! *(*DAD *slams the door shut, exiting)*

GARCIA: *(Comes out of the closet)* Fuck, dude. You gotta put up a fight. I mean, come on.

TEENAGE MALVO: I dunno, Garcia. I think he's coked up.

GARCIA: I mean, he's certainly on something. He's a ticking time bomb.

TEENAGE MALVO: I'm scared.

GARCIA: Hey, every son stands up to his father. It's part of becoming a man, right? So stand up, Malvo. Stand up!

TEENAGE MALVO: I've been booted outta my house since I was thirteen, fourteen, fifteen. I've slept on the front porch, freezing my ass off. All the fucking rain. And I look inside and he's all nice and cozy. So I tap on the window and he tells me to "Get ouuuuuuuuuuuuuut!" But don't worry 'bout him. He doesn't know anything about my friends. He's never met them. You're actually the first person to stay the night. I talk too much, don't I? I'm sorry. Do you want something to eat?

GARCIA: I'd love something to eat.

TEENAGE MALVO: Ok, why don't you get back in the closet and I'll get you a little breakfast?

GARCIA: Allright. *(Hides in the closet)*

TEENAGE MALVO: *(Yells offstage)* Dad! Dad! *(*DAD *enters)* It's the next day. You haven't fed me yet.

DAD: So?

TEENAGE MALVO: So it's time for breakfast. I'm hungry.

DAD: Steal some food.

TEENAGE MALVO: I haven't eaten anything. I haven't had lunch, I haven't had dinner. It's been days. Could you please…?

DAD: In a minute, in a minute! Wait just a little bit longer. And you'll get extra. Double portions. *(Takes off his shoe)* You feelin' feisty, Malvo?

TEENAGE MALVO: I just want something to eat. For the love of God, feed me!

DAD: All we got is a sack of brown sugar.

TEENAGE MALVO: Brown sugar? What?

DAD: We got brown sugar or nothing.

TEENAGE MALVO: You know what? That's fucking great. Let's be poor, let's be hungry. Let's go out and live on the street. You know, Dad, I'm starving, right? Right?

DAD: You want me to cook? *(Throws his shoe at* TEENAGE MALVO*, who ducks)* Cook what?

TEENAGE MALVO: Yeah, fucking cook for me. You call yourself a father? You say you love me? Well, cook something.

DAD: Eat my shoe! *(Chases* TEENAGE MALVO *around the room, brandishing his shoe)*

TEENAGE MALVO: You said you had my meals covered, right?

DAD: Shut up, Malvo.

GARCIA: *(Within the closet)* You shut up!

DAD: Nobody likes you. You don't even like yourself. Your own mother despises you.

GARCIA: *(Within the closet)* Hey, I do! I like Malvo. Stop saying evil shit.

DAD: You're so fuckin' stupid, you couldn't even sharpen a pencil. Your teacher showed you how. You fuckin' think you're gonna graduate high school? Just drop out, kid.

GARCIA: *(Within the closet)* You shouldn't talk to him that way. I mean, he didn't do anything wrong. He's not a bad kid, you're a bad father.

DAD: This is why you get stepped on! *(Throws his shoe at* TEENAGE MALVO *again)* Walked all over!

GARCIA: *(Within the closet)* Get mad!

DAD: 'Cause you keep opening your fuckin' mouth! *(Slaps* TEENAGE MALVO)

GARCIA: *(Within the closet)* Hit him back! Hard!

TEENAGE MALVO: Please! I can't take it anymore. *(*DAD *hits* TEENAGE MALVO *with his shoe)* STOP! Goddamn it!

DAD: Stop what?

GARCIA: *(Within the closet)* Let him go, you fuckin' prick!

TEENAGE MALVO: *(Whispers)* Stay in the closet, Garcia. You're talking too loud. Stay in the fucking closet.

GARCIA: *(Within the closet)* No, I'm coming out. *(Comes out of the closet)* Hey, you! You got no right to smack him around. I mean, look in his eyes. The light's gone. He's checked out. Don't you see that? How the hell does that not bother you?

TEENAGE MALVO: *(Disconnected)* Dad, this is my friend Garcia. Don't fuck with him, he's insane-o.

GARCIA: I'm a wild man. *(*DAD *rushes* TEENAGE MALVO*)* Come on, motherfucker! *(Slaps* DAD*)*

DAD: *(Stunned)* Malvo! Malvo! It's me! Your dad.

TEENAGE MALVO: *(Blandly)* Don't talk to me, talk to Garcia. *(*GARCIA *kicks* DAD *in the knee)*

DAD: Owwww! That hurt. Who taught you to fight dirty?

TEENAGE MALVO & GARCIA: You did.

DAD: Allright, that's it! I'm tired of your shit, Malvo. *(Unfolds a knife)*

GARCIA: *(Lifts his gun)* Stay back!

TEENAGE MALVO: Don't do it, Garcia.

GARCIA: *(Aims at* DAD*)* It's a long gun. It likes to shoot.

DAD: I'll stab you in the balls, kid.

TEENAGE MALVO: Don't do it. *(Swats the gun and it goes off, killing* DAD *instantly. The lights flash.* GARCIA *transitions into* TEENAGE MALVO, *who now holds the smoking gun, standing over* DAD. *A dramatic shadow is cast behind* TEENAGE MALVO*)* What's up now, kid? *(Pants heavily)*

SCENE 6

MALVO HILL JUNIOR, *under a spotlight*

MALVO HILL JUNIOR: *(To the audience)* After Malvo shot and killed his father, he was sentenced to three years by a juvenile court. On November 26th, 1998, Malvo reentered society a different person. In fact, he ran for mayor of Denver. I'm serious. Yeah, he opened his first campaign office on Colfax Avenue. He was a young man who had only begun to taste life.

SCENE 7

Morning. Outside "Savino's Fine Jewelry" store on Colfax Avenue. MALVO *wheezes.* TONY *walks up*

TONY: What's your fuckin' problem?
MALVO: Colfax. *(Moans)*
TONY: Well, let's go. Wake your ass up.
MALVO: Sleep. What is it? I haven't had it in so long.
TONY: Come on, you bum. Get up! Move it! You can't be here.
MALVO: Allright, chill your dick, man. You ever sleep on concrete? The sidewalk is unforgiving. It absorbs your body heat. Wrenches your back.
TONY: Yeah, well, you're trespassing. This is private property.
MALVO: I'm looking for a job. I came yesterday, but you didn't have any openings. So I spent the night here, to be first in line.
TONY: Look, man. Savino's Fine Jewelry has a strict "no bums" policy. Bums. Bad for business!
MALVO: Well, I'm not a bum. Please, hire me.
TONY: Forget it. I hire you and you turn around and tell all your slacker friends. And after that, there's no getting rid of you beggars. Now, I'm not gonna to tell you again. You're blocking my entrance. Move!
MALVO: I have nowhere to go. No bed to sleep in.
TONY: I don't care. Check into a shelter. You come in here, expecting me to put you on the list? Not a chance.
MALVO: That's very charitable, sir. Thank you.
TONY: Man, listen, the cure for poverty is work. That's it. You wanna generate money? You work for it. A magical cure.
MALVO: Hey, I'll do whatever. Whatever pays.
TONY: You mean dressed like that? Did Goodwill have a sale?
MALVO: I wish I could afford Goodwill, or a phone, or transportation. I

need money for that. But to get money, I need a job. So I got nothin'. I got no shoes. No food. I'm starving.

TONY: Eat garbage!

MALVO: Yeah, you try it for a day.

TONY: Pass. I'm not a homeless crackhead.

MALVO: Hey, I don't smoke crack.

TONY: Show me your glass-dick, come on. Where's it at? I know you get down.

MALVO: No, I really don't. I'm clean.

TONY: Clean? You live in a dumpster. You scavenge. You're a trashcan-rat.

MALVO: Dude, one just bit me. Yeah! Right before you got here. A huge rat just bit me right on my ass. See the teeth marks?

TONY: Oh, a rat did that, huh?

MALVO: *(Pants)* Nasty. *(Makes a guttural noise)*

TONY: Dude, you're a grown-ass man. You should be fuckin' that rat up!

MALVO: Nah, not me. I'm too skinny. *(Pants heavily)*

TONY: Yeah, 'cause you smoke that rock. *(We hear a beatbox)*

MALVO: *(Raps over the beat)* One, two, one, two. Check it, check it, check it. I dyed my pubic hairs blue. I spike my hair with glue. Never tie my shoes. Look, man, I can't lose. Take a fuckin' listen. Turn off your television. What, you again, hooligan? I'll yank out your teeth, so you can't yell "Police." Yeah, deflate your prostate. Break your nose. Throw a few body blows. Wiggle your toes. If your brain is froze. You old-timer with Alzheimer's.

TONY: Your nose — it's growing. Pointier and pointier.

MALVO: *(Hisses)* Yeah, and?

TONY: And your voice is changing too. You're turning into a street rat!

MALVO: Hah! I feel good, real good. I feel fully alive!

TONY: Whoa, whoa, whoa, back up, man. You're way too close. I can smell the skeez from here. *(We hear car horns)*

MALVO: Mmmmmm. *(We hear more car horns)* Mmmmmm. Who's that?

TONY: The Mayor, that's who.

MALVO: The Mayor of Denver?

TONY: Crossing Colfax, yeah. *(MAYOR enters, followed by* REPORTERS *with microphones)*

MAYOR: *(Into the microphone)* Hello! *(Brightly)* Good morning to you! Here I am, standing on America's longest, safest avenue. On the new Colfax. That's right! Colfax is making a comeback. A big comeback. No more homicides. No stray bullets, hitting the 15. None of that, now that I'm mayor. Now that I represent you. *(We hear car alarms)* Colfax! Denver's most famous street, remade. *(We hear a police siren)*

MALVO: Mayor, Mayor, Mayor! People, people, people! Please, please, please! *(Growls)*

TONY: This guy right here. Get away from him. He's crazy, mentally disturbed. All shaky and shit. You don't wanna talk to him.

MAYOR: Oh, I'll talk to anyone. I'm open to the public. Listen, I'm his Mayor too.

TONY: He's dangerous. Look! Look! He's foaming at the mouth.

MAYOR: Hey. No judgements here.

MALVO: *(Intensely)* That rat, that rat made my mouth water. It made my tongue drip. *(Pants heavily)*

TONY: See? Look. He's hypersalivating. He caught the shrew flu. It jumped from animal to person. Shit, he's carrying a deadly virus.

MAYOR: Listen, I have a plan. Wait until you hear it. My homeless outreach program.

TONY: Yeah, thanks, I've heard. You're moving all the lil' sickies up Colfax. Up but not out. You're just dumping 'em here. Like this bag of filth. Not even a trashman would pick him up.

MAYOR: That's not true.

MALVO: Nobody has any love for me? *(Has severe trouble breathing)*

MAYOR: Awww! Let me take you to a hospital.

MALVO: No, I'm too sick to go to the hospital.

MAYOR: Oh, you poor thing.

MALVO: You wanna hear my healthcare plan? I stay away from doctors! Much more affordable. *(Gurgles)*

MAYOR: Ok. Are you sure?

MALVO: You can't save me. It's too late.

MAYOR: They've got clean beds, TV and free food. Doesn't that sound great?

MALVO: Yeah, no, sounds suspicious.

MAYOR: Well, I guess what they say is true. You can judge a society by the health of the least among us. *(We hear five seconds of marching band music)*

MALVO: Hear me now.

MAYOR: Today, I look across the faces before me and I see a sad state of affairs.

MALVO: No, I said lemme speak.

MAYOR: Our reality is grim, but it is not hopeless.

MALVO: Here. Lemme speak into the microphone.

MAYOR: Please! Speak. I'm very interested in your thoughts.

MALVO: *(Into the microphone)* People, people, people! Vote Malvo Hill for mayor! I promise a newly-infected rat in every home. I promise a contaminated pigeon in every pot.

MAYOR: Ok, ok. No.

MALVO: Yes! Yes! And you know what else? I'm for global warming. The planet is overpopulated and overexploited. Too many people, too little resources. Some of the weaker and defective have gotta go.

MAYOR: Ah, I'm not sure I agree with that.

MALVO: Shut up! *(We hear a beatbox)* The only rule of the jungle is, I eat you. *(Raps over the beat)* Argh! Guess what? Your Mayor's a slut. She's open to gropin'. She says, "Well, hello." Then gives you a grab-n-go.

MAYOR: *(Raps over the beat)* Hey, I'm taking alot of abuse. From a guy with no front tooth. You think you own the street? Because this is where you sleep and eat?

MALVO: *(Raps over the beat)* The Mayor don't ask, she orders. But everyone ignores her. Elect me and I promise, I'll raze the city, the day I take office. And at my meet-and-greet, I'll tear it down, street by street. 'Cause I'm 'core. Life's amusing and, blah, it's a bore.

MAYOR: Come on, people. We can do better. I'm here, right here. I am listening. Answering your questions. That's how this works!

MALVO: What 'bout me, Mayor? Can I have a blanket? Excuse me! I'm part of the neighborhood. Can I have some water?

TONY: Go on, now! Throw him out!

MALVO: Is there any place I can fill my water bottle?

TONY: Just leave! You lil' nuisance.

MALVO: Please, have a heart. Gimme some help.

MAYOR: Be nice and I'll help you.

TONY: Clear the hell out! Some of us work for a living!

MALVO: *(Pants heavily)* Can I just fill this bottle?

MAYOR: I can get him some water. Hold on a second. You know, he's not asking for anything we can't give. He's not asking for money or food or a handout, so why make him suffer? I mean, water is a basic human right. It's actually against the law to deny people water.

TONY: Colfax bums! Who needs 'em?

MAYOR: All human beings are legally bound to have fresh water. I'll get him some. I'll be a friend like that. Here you go, sir. Here's a big jug.

MALVO: Thanks, Mayor. That's nice. *(Drinks water)*

MAYOR: Ok. Would you like hot tea with a lemon wedge? *(*MALVO *breathes slower)*

TONY: *(Taps the microphone)* This is a public service announcement! *(Into the microphone)* Stay away from the glass-penis, kids. You don't wanna to end up like this bummo. *(Kicks* MALVO, *who rages)* He's bugging out. Look at him.

MAYOR: What's wrong? Tell me. I want to understand.

MALVO: *(Gnashes his teeth)* Ugh, I'm dying here!

MAYOR: Well, if you're homeless, the City of Denver will take care of your cremation. Up to twenty-five-hundred dollars. Over twenty-five, they, uh, pull that money. Your burial costs, will they exceed twenty-five-hundred?

*(*MALVO *laughs maniacally)*

TONY: Watch out, Mayor! He's blood-crazy. Don't go near him. (MALVO *bites* MAYOR, *who screams in pain)*

MAYOR: Oh my God, he bit my hand, hard! And he won't let go.

TONY: Feed the bite, Mayor, feed the bite!

MAYOR: What do you mean, feed the bite?!

TONY: Push your hand into his mouth. Force his jaw open.

MAYOR: Ah! Great. Aah! Thanks.

TONY: Are you bleeding?

MAYOR: Yeah! But I'm ok. It's not the first time I've been bitten. *(Giggles)*

TONY: You think it's funny? *(*MAYOR *giggles more)* Seriously, if it can happen to the Mayor, it can happen to anyone. *(*MAYOR *giggles hysterically)*

MAYOR: I mean, really!

TONY: Mayor. This is no laughing matter.

MAYOR: *(Laughs uncontrollably)* Laughter's contagious!

TONY: So's rabies. *(*MALVO *barks)* Look! His eyes are rolling. Look!

MAYOR: Guess I'll go get tested and treated now. Um, yeah, no big deal.

TONY: *(*MALVO *spits on* TONY'S *suit jacket)* Jesus. Mayor, are you ok?

MAYOR: Oh, I'm fine.

TONY: You don't feel a little, uh, hostile?

MAYOR: No, I said I'm fine. Just thirsty. *(Pants heavily)*

TONY: Your face! It's changing. You're transmogrifying.

MAYOR: Yaaaaaaaoooooooowwll!

TONY: Damn, the incubation period is quick. *(*MAYOR *bites* TONY, *who screams in pain)* What? What? Now you're biting me? Hey!

MAYOR: *(Harshly)* Yeah. I bit you, so what? *(Growls)*

TONY: So I'm a voter. I pay property taxes. I own my small business. And I can't get any work done! *(*MAYOR *and* MALVO *growl.* REPORTERS *scatter)*

TONY: Help! Help! Please! I'm being attacked! Help me! Anyone there? Am I the only sane person left in this city? *(Growls)*

MALVO: *(In a low voice)* You look like me, you talk like me, you are me. A low-status bum. *(We hear a beatbox)* And Savino's Fine Jewelry is not a respecter of bums. *(Raps over the beat)* Ok, that's my terrible parable. The premise? In a brief sentence? Come down from the sky, big guy. Could be you in a year or two. Clawing back to the top. A boot to the tooth. Thanks alot. You're a big bunch of assholes. You locked me outta your households. You closed your doors to me. That's life in the big city. Denver left me so sickly. Where I'm at, I'm at the Cold Facts.

SCENE 8

MALVO HILL JUNIOR, *under a spotlight*

MALVO HILL JUNIOR: *(To the audience)* That's Malvo Hill. Spreading ideas and saliva. My phlegmy friend was angry. The people loved it. They're angry too. Malvo told some hard truths. Some cold facts. *(Paces)* Hey. Hey, draw the spotlight closer. Closer. The year is 2004. Malvo is twenty-five. He wants a rare item… but he doesn't wanna pay for it. Easier to steal than to earn, right?

SCENE 9

TONY SAVINO'S *jewelry store. Above it, his condo. The alleyway is also visible.* TONY *is behind the counter.* MALVO *gazes at the diamonds. We hear a cash register ringing, then a police bulletin*

OFFICER KLUNT: *(Voice-over)* BOLO! Be on the lookout! Jewel thief! White male. Brown hair, close-cropped. Medium build. Scarred complexion. Attempt to ID. Real name: Malvo Hill. Alias: Float Boy.
(We hear radio static)
MALVO: *(Voice-over)* Yeah, yeah! I'm a housebreaker. I sneak in through an open window, unlock your safe, then leave without a trace.
OFFICER KLUNT: *(Voice-over)* Five-foot-nine, a hundred-and-eighty pounds. Last seen wearing a particolored sweatshirt, backpack and red Converse-style high tops.
MALVO: *(Voice-over)* I rob old ladies 'cause they don't fight back. Well, I wait for 'em to go out, at least. If they come home, I just slide down a pipe. Perform a daring leap.
OFFICER KLUNT: *(Voice-over)* Malvo Hill is described as feral, with a lumpy head, whose current address is an abandoned warehouse. In addition to being armed, he is a deranged individual, who is prone to violent outbursts.
MALVO: *(Voice-over)* This one old bat, I'll never forget her. She looked blind, you know, but she saw me. She saw me lift her cigarette purse, while she washed dishes in her kitchen. *(We hear running water, then glass breaking)* She spun around, swinging a meat ax! And chased me out. *(We hear a rat hissing)* Oh, she hurt me badly. I ran out the back door and slammed it shut. *(We hear a door shut)* I got away, 'cause she couldn't turn the doorknob with soap all over her hands, you know. Heh, heh, heh… Yeah, I learned from her that sometimes little old ladies fight back. And they got unusually sharp teeth.

OFFICER KLUNT: *(Voice-over)* Situation: PD is attempting to locate a suspect in association with a string of home robberies that took place across the city in recent weeks.
MALVO: *(Voice-over)* Yeah, yeah! I score big dressed as a contract painter, carrying my ladder. Working out in the open, in full view. I'm into ladders. Mine's twenty-feet-tall. But I can fold it up, you know, it's transportable. My office hours are 8:00 to 4:00, Monday through Friday.
OFFICER KLUNT: *(Voice-over)* At 11:00, the individual in question fell out of a second-story bedroom window. Home occupant reported a rare cut-gem missing. Widely known as the rat's eye opal. Other jewelry and cash also taken. Arriving deputies were notified by the victim, one Tony Savino, that Malvo Hill broke into his condo, situated above his diamond business.
TONY: *(Notices* MALVO*)* Oh no, not this guy.
MALVO: Hello, Tony.
TONY: Can I help you?
MALVO: You like ice? I got diamonds. I'm a hopeful seller. You set diamonds, right?
TONY: Well, yeah.
MALVO: Then I came to the right dealer.
TONY: Fine. Why don't you sit down. Over there. And we can get down to bidness. *(We hear diamonds clinking)*
MALVO: I picked this outta the trash.
TONY: Damn — coming in here with this fatty ring.
MALVO: That's a two-point-eight carat. Let's trade. The ring for a bag of cash. A generous bag. I'll sell it for fifty-thousand dollars.
TONY: Nah, I wanna good deal, sonny.
MALVO: How 'bout this? A nine carat crucifix, Tony, for a quarter mil.
TONY: A quarter million? What are you, crazy? *(We hear high-pitched drilling)*
MALVO: Please! Turn that down.

TONY: Get lost. Can't you see I'm working here?

OFFICER KLUNT: *(Voice-over)* Distinguishing marks. Inner wrist: tattoo of figure in fedora hat and trench coat.

TONY: That tattoo — who is that? The Neighborhood Watch guy who's crossed out on all the signs?

MALVO: Uh-huh.

TONY: You branded yourself a criminal?

MALVO: No, I just identify with this character.

TONY: Well, you deserve to get caught if you're that stupid. *(We hear more high-pitched drilling)*

MALVO: So… how 'bout this? *(Unzips a pouch)* A gold bar. Twenty-seven grams.

TONY: Ok, you can call that a bullion, if you want to. But I call it a cheap yellow brick.

MALVO: It's a hundred percent pure gold. Look what I brought you.

TONY: No, yeah, sure, right. Soft gold. Soft and heavyweight. *(We hear a telephone ringing)*

MALVO: Are you gonna get that?

TONY: Savino's Fine Jewelry.

OFFICER KLUNT: *(Voice-over)* Can I speak to Tony Savino?

TONY: Speaking.

OFFICER KLUNT: *(Voice-over)* Hello. This is Officer Klunt with the Denver Police Department.

TONY: Yeah, so?

OFFICER KLUNT: *(Voice-over)* Unfortunately, the building manager at your condominium called us, sir, and reported suspicious activity. He discovered the door to your unit unsecured. Someone forced their way in. I'm sorry for the bad news.

TONY: No, no. I didn't hear nothin'. And I live right above my shop.

OFFICER KLUNT: *(Voice-over)* Do you have valuables at home? In your safe?

TONY: Ahh, Christ! *(Hangs up)* What a goddamn day. *(*MALVO *looks down)* Hey, you, we're closed.

MALVO: Where am I supposed to go? A big snowstorm hit and I'm homeless.

TONY: So? Nobody wants you here! Go on! Get outta my shop, you stupid animal. *(*MALVO*, cornered, scratches* TONY*)* Aww, Jesus! You really got me! *(We hear a shop doorbell.* TONY *kicks out* MALVO*, who exits)* You mamaluc, ya. *(Locks his shop, then climbs the stairs to his condo. We hear street noise)* Don't tell me, don't tell me it's gone. Not my rat's-eye ring and the rest of the purple gems. Please, Mother of God, no! *(At his front door)* Ok, nobody broke my locks. My front door's intact. What the hell's going on? *(We hear a police bulletin)*

OFFICER KLUNT: *(Voice-over)* The same suspect was captured on home security video at the victim's residence.

TONY: I don't even have a damn building manager. So who's making false reports? *(Closely examines his safe)* Huh. *(Turns the dial)* Are my stones in here? *(Opens his safe)* Let's pray. *(Breathes a sigh of relief)* There you are, come here… Mwah, mwah, mwah… I love you forever… My precious, precious opal… Mwah, mwah, mwah… *(*MALVO *enters from the balcony)*

MALVO: Excuse my interruption.

TONY: *(Gasps)* What the fuck? Who let you in?

MALVO: Me? I picked your lock. Came in through the back.

TONY: Unannounced?

MALVO: Yeah. I followed you here.

TONY: You gotta be fuckin' kidding. I don't believe it.

MALVO: Believe it. The police did.

TONY: The police?

MALVO: Over the phone. I posed as the building manager. Right before I stepped into your shop. Yeah, that was me. I set you up.

TONY: Why?

MALVO: What's the combination to your safe?

TONY: I'm not telling you that.

MALVO: That's why. *(Cocks his gun)*

TONY: Oh, you're strapped, too, huh?

MALVO: Gimme the opal. Kiss-ss-ss it goodbye, Tony, for the last time.

TONY: You sneaky fuck… *(Hands his rat's eye opal to* MALVO*)* You realize I'm gonna to find your ass.

MALVO: *(His gun jams)* …dammit…

TONY: *(Screams)* I want you outta my house… *(Rushes* MALVO*)* …right now! *(Pushes* MALVO *out of his window. We hear breaking glass, then a body drop)*

MALVO: *(Offstage)* Yaaaaaaaaaah! *(*TONY *picks up a phone and dials. We hear ringing)*

OFFICER KLUNT: *(Voice-over)* Officer Klunt.

TONY: Officer Klunt. This is Tony Savino, calling you back. I have an emergency. My address is 1890 South Emerson Street. I'm reporting the commission of a crime. An armed home invasion. *(Pause)* I lost my most valuable gem. A purple opal. I'm a jeweler. This kid was in my shop not ten minutes ago, trying to sell me a hot diamond crucifix. Now I discover him in my bedroom. *(Pause)* Yeah, just now. Please send help!

OFFICER KLUNT: *(Voice-over)* The intruder, is he still on your property?

TONY: No. I pushed him outta my window, after he sprang on top of me. I'm looking down on him. Aww, Jesus Christ. Both his legs are cracked and he's bleeding in the alley. On a big snow mound. It broke his fall.

OFFICER KLUNT: *(Voice-over)* Well, don't go near him, sir.

TONY: Then come pick him up. Fuck! Look in the back alley.

OFFICER KLUNT: *(Voice-over)* I'm pulling into your parking lot now. — Dispatch, we got a live one here. A 10-91c.

TONY: *(Hangs up, then screams out of his window)* You landed on your back.

It was that brick — it weighed you down. Yeah, that brick in your pocket.

MALVO: *(Offstage)* Oh God. (*Cries out in pain*) No brick, no trick. I got magic gold.

TONY: *(Screams)* Allright, I'm coming down, but it better be real magic gold. *(Walks down his steps)* Shit, you don't rob me, I rob you. *(Cocks* MALVO'S *gun)* Yeah, how do you like me now?

MALVO: *(Offstage)* I didn't like you before.

TONY: Quiet! Before I blast you with your own piece. (*Drags* MALVO *on-stage*) This is a blind alley. Open only at one end.

MALVO: *(Strains)* Please, no more. Take what you want — it's yours. Just don't hurt me.

TONY: Allright, where the fuck's my opal? Huh? *(Digs into* MALVO'S *pockets)* Give it up. I'm not gonna tell you again. Give it up!

MALVO: In-between my teeth.

TONY: Yeah? Show me. Show me your toothiest smile. I wanna see fuckin' sparkles. *(We hear sparks igniting)* Hey, hey, hey. Stop fuckin' around, huh? *(We hear police sirens wailing)* Outta luck, alley rat. *(We hear a patrol car pulling up)* Hey, how youse doin'? I'm over here. Tony Savino. I disarmed him. *(Drags* MALVO *offstage. We hear police radio chatter, then handcuffs clicking)* Threw his weapon into that dumpster. Yes, Mr. Officer, sir. *(*OFFICER KLUNT *enters)*

OFFICER KLUNT: *(Into his walkie-talkie)* Suspect arrested. Malvo Hill is no longer a threat to the community. *(We hear high-pitched whirring, then handcuffs unhooking)*

MALVO: *(Offstage)* That's what you think, fuck-os. Ha, ha! *(We hear a police bulletin)*

OFFICER KLUNT: *(Looks offstage)* Damn. *(Into his walkie-talkie)* Be alert! The vicious criminal known as Malvo Hill has escaped police custody. *(*TONY *enters)*

TONY: *(Loses his mind)* Why!! Why does this shit always happen to me?

OFFICER KLUNT: *(Into his walkie-talkie)* All units in the area, respond to the southeast corner of Emerson and Downing. Officers seeking fugitive.
TONY: My purple opal! Noo-ooo-ooo!
OFFICER KLUNT: *(Into his walkie-talkie)* Suspect was handcuffed, but used a microdrill, possibly an electrified jeweler's tool, to cut a small hole under the hook. NFI! No further information.

SCENE 10

MALVO HILL JUNIOR, *under a spotlight*

MALVO HILL JUNIOR: *(To the audience)* Tony's opal. That was a thing of beauty. Opals are iridescent. They reflect a million complementary colors. This one flashed dollar signs. We checked into the Brown Palace Hotel. Celebrated the joys of room service. English tea and scones. It was a fucking great time. We partied from early in the morning to late at night. One day, the hotel manager banged on the door and asked Malvo to turn down the music. Malvo told him, "Fuck your request, I'm the guest." Ha, ha!! I'll never meet another person like Malvo Hill. Ever since he died, the breadcrumbs don't taste the same. The peach pits aren't as sweet. *(Leans forward)* Uhhhh, you're telling me to go where? You mean get trampled? No! I'm not goin' nowhere. I'm hiding from sight, deep in the shadows. *(Pause)* No, uh-uh, never. Never! Never! *(Pause)* Why would I? I'm all cozed out. *(Pause)* Ok, maybe you're right. Maybe I should find new grounds to burrow in. I should just shut up and do it. Plug my rathole. I've been down here so long, just plotting my revenge on society. *(Pause)* Never. Never been to the roof. Never looked down. Never seen Denver. Be the first time. *(Pause)* Huh? You wanna go up there? Take in the view? Then get cheese-drunk and pass out on a block of cheddar? That would be rad. *(Stands up)* Thanks for listening to me. You're actually pretty nice. *(In a New York accent)* Come on, let's go to Wash Park and break some kneecaps, huh? *(Crawls out of his rathole)* Ha, ha!! *(Looks around)* Hey, ya got any snacks?

End of Play

ROSE
SECURITY

GHOST OF UNION STATION

CAST OF CHARACTERS

LEO PERINO *54 years old, a security guard*

ROSE LIPSTEIN *35 years old, a housewife*

RADIO HOST

PLACE

Union Station. Denver, Colorado

TIME

Halloween, 1949 & 2026

SCENE

The basement of Union Station. "Night on Bald Mountain" by Modest Mussorgsky plays and quickly fades out

RADIO HOST: *(Voice-over)* Welcome, everyone, to the Union Station Radio Show! Thanks for joining me on this fine evening. (SOUND: *applause)* Our performance is being recorded live at Union Station, on 17th Avenue, in downtown Denver. I love bare mountain air, don't you? (SOUNDS: *train whistles, then rumbles overhead)* So good to be with you from this modernized lobby. I'm the host of tonight's broadcast. (MUSIC: "*Night on Bald Mountain" for ten seconds)* Right on, right on. We're going to memory lane it now. Tell a story of Old Denver, and reveal the secret history of Union Station. I promise to bring you a spooky-dooky Halloween. Oh, there will be a beautiful woman in distress, an unsuspecting guard, and mini-mole people. Yes! (SOUND: *Mole people chatter)* Mini-mole people! Pocket-sized! They spy on Rose and Leo from the lower depths of Union Station. Just wait and see. We're living in the 2020's, but mental time travel back to the 1940's. Yeah, it's the '40s. That's right. 1949, in fact. The Second World War is over. Denver City is booming. Ten-thousand people a day travel through Union Station. Now let's go down deep into the basement. Ah yeah, under the rails. Mmwhaa-ha-ha-ha-ha! It's time to kick off the show! A seasonal production of Mark Sbani's "Ghost of Union Station." (MUSIC: *"Night on Bald Mountain" for ten seconds.* ROSE *enters)*

ROSE: Ssst! Are you the night watchman?

LEO: *(Enters)* Oh. I didn't see you there. You snuck up on me. Hello, I'm Officer Leo Perino. What's your name?

ROSE: Rose Lipstein.

LEO: Rose. How can I help you?

ROSE: Please, come a little closer. Get over here.

LEO: Ma'am, the platform's this way. Up the stairs.

ROSE: They cancelled it. The midnight service to Black Hawk. A tunnel closed. Or thick fog.
LEO: So you came down here. Why?
ROSE: *(Very quietly)* I heard something: voices. Drunken hobos, screaming at each other.
LEO: You heard voices in the basement?
ROSE: Transients. When I turned the corner, they vanished. They went poof! Now look for the trespassers, Officer Perino. Duty calls.
LEO: Nobody's allowed in this area. It's restricted. Been closed all year, due to a wrongful death.
ROSE: Did I hear you say "Due to wrongful death?" Well, that's significant.
LEO: How so?
ROSE: Well, someone died, didn't they? On your watch. Are you even paying attention? You're giving me cow eyes.
LEO: Look, I'm just going to say this. Whatever happened, it happened one year ago, tonight. (SOUND: *heavy footsteps)* Allright. Well, I don't see anything. No unusual activity. Twenty-three-forty-five on October 31st, 1949. Let's go back upstairs, huh?
ROSE: I can't. My husband, Ed, is waiting for me in the lobby. Ed thinks I wronged him. That I two-timed him with his bowling buddy. So I'm hiding. Hiding from Ed. He is an insanely jealous man. I walked out on him, but he followed me here. Down to the tracks. His name is Ed Rossi, Officer. Put that in your report. Ed Rossi.
LEO: Eddie Spaghetti. With ravioli eyes and a meatball head.
ROSE: You kind of look like him, you know. You're both skinny Italians.
LEO: As a matter of fact, I'm full-blooded Italian. Four-fourths.
ROSE: Andiamo, Leo. Andiamo. Let's go. Move it.
LEO: Look, all I see are black walls and you: an insurance liability.
ROSE: Ever fraternize with the public, Ed? I mean, Leo.
LEO: Of course not. That's against protocol. (MUSIC: *"Night on*

Bald Mountain")

ROSE: *(Delighted)* Oooh! Devilish music on a Saturday night.

LEO: Where the hell is that coming from? Who's really down here?

ROSE: Well, Leo, if you go looking, you'll find it. *(More* MUSIC: *"Night on Bald Mountain")* Do you ride the lines often?

LEO: Never.

ROSE: Never? I mean, not even once? (MUSIC *cuts)*

LEO: No. I prefer to use my own two feet. I'm prone to train-sickness, you know. All that bouncing around? While you're eating a meal? No!

ROSE: Come this way. Be quick.

LEO: Where? Where are we going? We're halfway to Black Hawk, Rose.

ROSE: Goddamn Union Station. They cancelled Black Hawk. I'll never board that train.

LEO: Rose, tell me about your husband. Ed. Talk more about him.

ROSE: *(Softly)* He put me in my grave and left me there. *(Loudly)* Now investigate! Patrol, guard, patrol!

LEO: I'm always on patrol. I don't know how to sit down. Mm, maybe I should investigate you. You said you left your husband, but where's your luggage? You heard voices. What, unbodied voices? Are they real or are they a diversion?

ROSE: What are you suggesting?

LEO: Look, I need to report back. It's time to turn in the keys. Sorry. (SOUNDS: *cacophony of cackles and snarls)* You hear that? Shhh! Listen! That's them, in the distance.

ROSE: Who?

LEO: Mole people.

ROSE: *(In disbelief)* Are you serious? Mole people?

LEO: Description: pink eyes, phosphorescent skin. Miniature humans who live underground. They hunt in packs. Little devils. They're watching us right now. I mean it, we're in real danger.

ROSE: Leo, your hands are shaking. Are you allright?

LEO: No, I'm petrified with fear.

ROSE: Let's do something heroic. Let's detain them. (SOUND: *more cackles)* You got a Union Station issued whistle, Leo, use it. (LEO *blows his whistle)* That's right! Blow it again.

LEO: *(Blows his whistle again)* Please stand back, Rose. A commuter railroad can be a dangerous environment. You ride at your own risk.

ROSE: Oh, I'm not afraid. Are you, Ed?

LEO: You seem to forget my name. I'm Leo Perino. I just met you. Strange, very strange. Calling me by your husband's name.

ROSE: Leo, turn around.

LEO: Why? Why are you so interested in me?

ROSE: I like you. I'm sorry.

LEO: But I don't understand why.

ROSE: I apologize. I suppose you hate me.

LEO: No, I just don't trust you. I never trust beautiful women.

ROSE: You don't?

LEO: And your name. You see, I'm allergic to roses. The flowers. Any color, under my nose, I get what's called rose fever.

RADIO HOST: *(Voice-over)* Attention! This is a security announcement. We ask you to avoid eye contact with the transients. Their mood has become dark. If you see something that isn't right, page the Night Watchman. Officer Leo Perino. He'll sort it out.

ROSE: You hear that, Ed? Sort it out.

LEO: Are you talking to me? (SOUND: *train passes overhead)*

ROSE: Eddddddd!

LEO: Fine. Call me anything you want.

ROSE: Oh, what's this? An old baggage car, huh? Go on, climb in. *(Opens a creaky metal door)*

LEO: Oh no, oh no. I'm not getting in there. I have a funny feeling.

ROSE: *(Whispers)* He lifted me up by the throat and crushed my larynx.

LEO: Rose, you speak too softly. I really can't hear you.

ROSE: And you speak too loudly. It's quiet in the baggage car.

RADIO HOST: *(Voice-over)* Paging Officer Perino! It's quarter to midnight. No one knows where the watchman is? Leo. Is he lost, or more crucially, is he missed?

ROSE: Leo, get in. I don't have time for this. Get inside. Now. (LEO *sighs, then climbs inside the baggage car)* Don't tell me how to live. And don't call me stupid. Or you'll be sorry, Ed.

LEO: I didn't say you were stupid. And I'm not these other men. We've been through this. I'm a courtly gentleman. Ask anyone.

ROSE: *(Bitterly)* You took me into the basement, Ed, then strangled and discarded me.

LEO: I never strangled anyone!

ROSE: You strangled me with one hand. Grasped my neck and squeezed. My chin is so small, it was easy. My half-a-chin didn't get in the way. My ch—.

LEO: Look, Rose, you're very upset. You have alot of emotional problems. I mean, everybody does.

ROSE: I don't have emotional problems! *(Slaps* LEO)

RADIO HOST: *(Voice-over)* As I said at the top of the show, she's troubled.

LEO: Hey! Are you crazy? You can't hit an Officer. That's felonious! (ROSE *slams the door shut. We hear it clang, then lock)* Hey, what's the big idea? The door. You slammed it in my face. *(Knocks on window)* Open the door, Rose! Open it! Did you lock me in? Rose, I can see you through the window. You shut me in!

ROSE: One year dead. I am one year dead, upon the hour.

LEO: Rose, you're not alive?

ROSE: Very observant, Leo. I'm a ghost and you disrespected me.

LEO: I disrespected you? Leo Perino? That doesn't sound like me.

ROSE: Last year, you were working the night shift. You were supposed to be guarding the lobby.

LEO: *(Terrified)* Allright, so take my badge. Don't take my life. Please! *(Pounds his fist on the door)* This is wrong! *(Furiously)* You don't trap people for no reason.

ROSE: You saw me and did nothing. You went limp, as Ed dragged me downstairs.

LEO: I don't remember that.

ROSE: *(Laments)* Well, I do. Those were my last moments. I died so miserably.

LEO: I'm sorry. I'm sorry. I wasn't paying attention.

ROSE: You get paid to pay attention. It was your duty to respond, Leo.

LEO: *(Panic-stricken)* Rose! It was an honest mistake. I learned my lesson. I'll never fall asleep on post again.

ROSE: You let me down, Leo. You owe me.

LEO: Owe you what?

ROSE: Your life, Ed.

LEO: I'm Leo! Leo Perino!

ROSE: This is for the cries of help that went ignored.

LEO: My heart is racing. I can't breathe. *(Whimpers)* Rose! *(Whimpers louder, scratching the door)* Rose!

ROSE: Awww, baby blue eyes.

LEO: That's a ghost talking. I'm ignoring her. I don't believe she exists.

ROSE: Oh, Leo. You're such a fool!

LEO: You can't just leave me here.

RADIO HOST: *(Voice-over)* What a bum-out, Leo. You're locked inside a baggage car, underground. You're totally fucked.

LEO: Rose! I'll arrest you for false imprisonment! What am I talking about? I'll arrest your husband, when I get out of here. I'll charge him with murder by strangulation.

ROSE: Ahhh! That's the correct answer. Arrest my husband.

LEO: Ok, then unlock this door, immediately!

ROSE: Here's a clue, detective. You hold the key to your own cell.

LEO: Uh, where is my master set? Do I have the baggage key or not? *(Jingles his keys, then uses one to turn the lock)* It fits. I'm free! *(Opens the metal door)* Oh, thank you, Lord! I'm loving life! *(Glances around)* Rose? Rose? Are you there?

ROSE: Well, Leo, I'd love to stay and chitchat, but I'm leaving. My train is pulling out. *(Exits)*

RADIO HOST: *(Voice-over)* May I have your attention. The midnight train to Black Hawk is back in service. The fog has dissipated, allowing us to see things clearly. All aboard! Boarding. (SOUND: *long applause)* Thank you very much. We really appreciate that. Ok, ladies and gentlemen, that's our program. This production was brought to you by friends at the Union Station Radio Show. Happy Halloween, people. Mmwhaa-ha-ha-ha-ha-ha-ha-ha.

End of Play

THE TRAGEDY AT MARSDON MANOR

An Adaption of Agatha Christie's Radio Play

CAST OF CHARACTERS

INSPECTOR HUFFINGTON *60 years old*

DENBY *52 years old*

MRS. MALTRAVERS *30 years old*

CAPTAIN BLACK *35 years old*

DR. BERNARD *47 years old*

GARDENER *39 years old*

PLACE

London, England

TIME

1923

SCENE

A stately mansion located in the West End of London

DENBY: Are you called away on a case, then, Huffington?
INSPECTOR HUFFINGTON: Yes, Denby. For the Northern Union Insurance Company. They asked me to investigate the death of Jack Maltravers. Evidently, he was on the verge of bankruptcy. Then, three weeks ago, he insured his life with Northern Union. There is, of course, the usual suicide clause in the policy. In the event of committing suicide, the premiums are forfeited. Mr. Maltravers was quite a healthy man. However, on Wednesday last — the day before yesterday — his body was found in his home at Marsdon Manor.
DENBY: Where's this Marsdon Manor?
INSPECTOR HUFFINGTON: Here in London.
DENBY: And the cause of death?
INSPECTOR HUFFINGTON: Some kind of internal hemorrhage. Maltravers had a beautiful young wife. It's been suggested that he got together all the money he could and paid the premiums on a life insurance, and then committed suicide… for his wife's benefit. Such a thing is not uncommon. In any case, the director of the insurance company asked me to investigate. Though I'm not very hopeful of success. If the cause of death had been heart failure, I'd be more optimistic. Heart failure means the local doctor couldn't say what his patient really died of. But a hemorrhage seems fairly definite.
DENBY: Yes, that's true.
INSPECTOR HUFFINGTON: Still! We can make some necessary inquires. We go at once. To Marsdon Manor!
SOUNDS: taxi pulls up, then takes them away
INSPECTOR HUFFINGTON: I've ascertained that there is only one doctor in Marsdon, Doctor Ralph Bernard. Ah, here we are at his house.

SOUNDS: doorbell rings, then a door opens

DR. BERNARD: Yes, yes? What's this all about?

INSPECTOR HUFFINGTON: Hello, Dr. Bernard. My name is Inspector Huffington. I'm looking into the death of Mr. Maltravers for the Northern Union Insurance Company.

DR. BERNARD: Of course, of course. Come inside. It's my consulting hour, and I have no patients waiting. I suppose, rich as he was, his life was insured for a big sum?

INSPECTOR HUFFINGTON: You consider him a rich man, Dr. Bernard?

DR. BERNARD: Was he not? Marsdon Manor is a pretty big place to keep up.

INSPECTOR HUFFINGTON: I understand he had considerable losses of late.

DR. BERNARD: Is that so? Well, it's fortunate for his wife, then, that there's life insurance. A very beautiful and charming young creature. But terribly unstrung. A mass of nerves, poor thing. I tried to spare her, but the shock was bound to be considerable.

INSPECTOR HUFFINGTON: Have you attended Mr. Maltravers recently?

DR. BERNARD: My dear sir, I've never attended him.

INSPECTOR HUFFINGTON: What?

DR. BERNARD: Mr. Maltravers was a Christian Scientist, or something of that kind. Part of a faith healing sect.

INSPECTOR HUFFINGTON: But you examined the body?

DR. BERNARD: Certainly. I was fetched by one of the gardeners.

INSPECTOR HUFFINGTON: And the cause of death was clear?

DR. BERNARD: Absolutely. There was blood on the lips. But most of the bleeding must have been internal.

INSPECTOR HUFFINGTON: The body had not been touched?

DR. BERNARD: No. He was lying at the edge of a farm. He evidently was out shooting crows. A long barrel bird-gun was found beside him. The hemorrhage must have occurred quite suddenly. Gastric ulcers, without a doubt.

INSPECTOR HUFFINGTON: No question of him being shot, eh?

DR. BERNARD: My dear sir! You won't find any bullet wounds on the body or head of Mr. Maltravers.

INSPECTOR HUFFINGTON: Did he have on his shoes?

DR. BERNARD: Yes. *(Clears his throat)* Now, if there's nothing further—

INSPECTOR HUFFINGTON: Many thanks to you, doctor. Just one more thing. You saw no need for an autopsy?

DR. BERNARD: Certainly not. The cause of death was clear. I saw no reason to distress the widow.

SOUND: door slams shut

DENBY: Rather an old ass.

INSPECTOR HUFFINGTON: Exactly, Denby. Your judgments of character are always profound, my friend.

DENBY: Thank you.

INSPECTOR HUFFINGTON: There is the question of the beautiful woman. The widow. Let's call on her at Marsdon Manor.

SOUNDS*:* taxi takes them away, then a doorbell rings

INSPECTOR HUFFINGTON: Here she comes. Her eyes are red with weeping. She is very fair.

DENBY: Aye, very fair indeed. With large blue eyes.

SOUND: front door opens

MRS. MALTRAVERS: Yes? Is it something about my husband's insurance?

INSPECTOR HUFFINGTON: I'm afraid so.

MRS. MALTRAVERS: Must I be bothered now? So soon?

INSPECTOR HUFFINGTON: Well, your late husband insured his life for rather a large sum. The insurance company has empowered me to act for them. Now, please. Will you recount the sad events of Wednesday?

MRS. MALTRAVERS: *(Sighing)* I was changing for tea when my maid came up. One of the gardeners had just ran to the house. He had found— *(Breaks down crying)*

INSPECTOR HUFFINGTON: Your husband — did you see him earlier in the afternoon?

MRS. MALTRAVERS: Not since lunch. I walked down to the village for some candles, and he was shooting crows.

INSPECTOR HUFFINGTON: Shooting crows, eh?

MRS. MALTRAVERS: Yes, he usually took his bird-gun with him. I heard one or two shots in the distance.

INSPECTOR HUFFINGTON: Where is his bird-gun now?

MRS. MALTRAVERS: In the hall, I think.

SOUND: INSPECTOR HUFFINGTON inspects the bird-gun

INSPECTOR HUFFINGTON: One shot fired, I see. Thank you. By the way, do you know anything about your husband's financial position?

MRS. MALTRAVERS: Nothing. I'm very stupid about business.

INSPECTOR HUFFINGTON: I see. Then you can give us no clue as to why he suddenly decided to insure his life? He had not done so previously, I understand.

MRS. MALTRAVERS: Well, we had only been married a little over a year. As to why? He made up his mind that he wouldn't live long. He had a strong premonition of his own death. He had one stroke already. He knew another one would prove fatal. I tried to dispel his gloom but, sadly, he was only too right! *(Cries)* Oh, I'll show you to the door.

INSPECTOR HUFFINGTON: Good day.

DENBY: Good day.

INSPECTOR HUFFINGTON: Well, that's that, my friend. There appears to be no mouse in this mouse-hole. And yet—

DENBY: Yet what?

INSPECTOR HUFFINGTON: A slight discrepancy, that's all. Life is full of discrepancies. Surely Maltravers couldn't have taken his own life. There's no poison that would fill his mouth with blood. No, no. This case is above-board.

SOUND: heavy footsteps

INSPECTOR HUFFINGTON: But who is this? Tell me, Gardener, who is that gentleman?

GARDENER: I don't remember his name, sir. He stayed here last week. Tuesday, it was.

INSPECTOR HUFFINGTON: He's retreating up the drive. Quick, let's follow him.

SOUND: light footsteps

MRS. MALTRAVERS: You? *(Gasps)* I thought you were at sea, on your way to East Africa?

CAPTAIN BLACK: I got some news from my lawyers that detained me. My uncle in Scotland died unexpectedly and left me some money. Then I saw this bad news in the paper and came down to see if I could do anything. You'll want someone to look after things a bit.

INSPECTOR HUFFINGTON: I'm sorry, I left my walking stick in the hall.

MRS. MALTRAVERS: Inspector Huffington, this is Captain Black.

INSPECTOR HUFFINGTON: Captain Black?

CAPTAIN BLACK: Aye, that's right.

INSPECTOR HUFFINGTON: Are you staying at Marsdon Manor?

CAPTAIN BLACK No, I'm putting up at the Anchor Inn.

INSPECTOR HUFFINGTON: Ah. Well, I don't see my missing stick. Apologies. Good day.

SOUND: withdrawing footsteps

INSPECTOR HUFFINGTON: Come, Denby. Let's make a bee line for the Anchor Inn. We'll engage a room until Captain Black returns. He was at Marsdon Manor on Tuesday night — the day before Mr. Maltravers died. We must carefully investigate the doings of Captain Black.

SOUND: theme music

INSPECTOR HUFFINGTON: There's our quarry. He's approaching the inn. Accost him, Denby, and bring him to our room.

DENBY: Presently.

SOUND: DENBY *grabs* CAPTAIN BLACK

DENBY: You're nicked. Come with me.

CAPTAIN BLACK: What's the meaning of this?

SOUND: door opens

INSPECTOR HUFFINGTON: Hello, Captain Black. May I have a word with you?

CAPTAIN BLACK: I suppose.

INSPECTOR HUFFINGTON: You seem very devoted to Mrs. Maltravers. Poor thing — she answered enough painful questions. No need to ask more. But! You were at Marsdon Manor just before the occurrence. You can give us valuable information. Such as Mr. Maltravers' state of mind.

CAPTAIN BLACK: I'll do anything I can to help you.

INSPECTOR HUFFINGTON: Thank you, young soldier.

CAPTAIN BLACK: Maltravers is a friend of my people's, but I didn't know him well myself. And I didn't notice anything out of the ordinary.

INSPECTOR HUFFINGTON: You came down — when?

CAPTAIN BLACK: Tuesday afternoon. I walked to town early Wednesday morning. My boat sailed about twelve o'clock. But some news I got made me alter my plans.

INSPECTOR HUFFINGTON: You were returning to East Africa, I understand?

CAPTAIN BLACK: Why, yes. I've been out there since the War. Great country.

INSPECTOR HUFFINGTON: Exactly. Now, what was the talk about at dinner on Tuesday night?

CAPTAIN BLACK: Oh, I don't know. The usual odd topics. Maltravers asked after my people, and then we discussed the question of German reparations. Mrs. Maltravers asked alot of questions about East Africa. I told them

one or two yarns. That's about all, I think.
INSPECTOR HUFFINGTON: Thank you. I'd like to try a little experiment, with your permission. You told us what your conscious self knows. Now I want to question your subconscious self.
CAPTAIN BLACK: *(Alarmed)* Psychoanalysis, what?
INSPECTOR HUFFINGTON: Oh, no. You see, it's like this. I give you a word. You answer with another, and so on. Any word. The first one you think of.
CAPTAIN BLACK: Very well.
INSPECTOR HUFFINGTON: Shall we begin?
CAPTAIN BLACK: Allright.
INSPECTOR HUFFINGTON: Note down the words, please, Denby. We will commence. Day.
CAPTAIN BLACK: Night.
INSPECTOR HUFFINGTON: Name.
CAPTAIN BLACK: Place.
INSPECTOR HUFFINGTON: Bernard.
CAPTAIN BLACK: Shaw.
INSPECTOR HUFFINGTON: Tuesday.
CAPTAIN BLACK: Dinner.
INSPECTOR HUFFINGTON: Journey.
CAPTAIN BLACK: Ship.
INSPECTOR HUFFINGTON: Country.
CAPTAIN BLACK: Uganda.
INSPECTOR HUFFINGTON: Story.
CAPTAIN BLACK: Lions.
INSPECTOR HUFFINGTON: Bird-gun.
CAPTAIN BLACK: Farm.
INSPECTOR HUFFINGTON: Shot.
CAPTAIN BLACK: Suicide.

INSPECTOR HUFFINGTON: Elephant.
CAPTAIN BLACK: Tusks.
INSPECTOR HUFFINGTON: Money.
CAPTAIN BLACK: Lawyers.
INSPECTOR HUFFINGTON: Thank you, Captain Black. Perhaps you could come back in a few minutes?
CAPTAIN BLACK: Certainly. I'll go to my room and unpack.
SOUND: door closes
INSPECTOR HUFFINGTON: You see, Denby? You see it all?
DENBY: I don't know what you mean.
INSPECTOR HUFFINGTON: That list of words tells you nothing? Scrutinize it.
DENBY: No, nothing.
INSPECTOR HUFFINGTON: I'll assist you. To begin with, Black answered well within the normal time limit, with no pauses. So! He has no guilty knowledge to conceal. "Day" to "Night" and "Place" to "Name" are normal associations. I began with "Bernard," suggesting the local doctor. Evidently, he had not come across him at all. Black gave "Dinner" to my "Tuesday," but "Journey" and "Country" were answered by "Ship" and "Uganda," showing his journey abroad was more important than the one which brought him here. "Story" recalled one of the "Lion" yarns he told at dinner. "Bird-gun" was answered with the totally unexpected word "Farm." When I said "Shot," he answered at once with "Suicide." The association seems clear. A man he knows committed suicide with a bird-gun on a farm somewhere. Remember, too, that his mind is still on the stories he told at dinner.
SOUNDS: theme music, then a door opens
INSPECTOR HUFFINGTON: Hello again, Captain Black. Thank you for returning so quickly. Can you repeat the particular suicide story which you told at the dinner table on Tuesday evening?
CAPTAIN BLACK: Yes, I did tell them that story, come to think of it. Chap

shot himself on a farm out there. Did it with a bird-gun through the roof of the mouth. Bullet lodged in his brain. Doctors were puzzled over it. Nothing to show but a little blood on the lips. But what — what has this got to do with—

INSPECTOR HUFFINGTON: You didn't know he was found with a bird-gun by his side?

CAPTAIN BLACK: You mean my story suggested to him — oh, but that's awful!

INSPECTOR HUFFINGTON: Don't get upset, Captain Black. It would've been one way or another. Well! I must get back to Marsdon Manor and break the news to the young widow. She'll be left penniless, with the knowledge that her husband had killed himself to assure her future. A hard burden for any woman to bear.

DENBY: Yes. Yes, our interview with the lady will be painful.

INSPECTOR HUFFINGTON: Well, let's get it over with, Denby.

SOUNDS: taxi takes them away, then a door opens

INSPECTOR HUFFINGTON: Mrs. Maltravers, I am so sorry.

MRS. MALTRAVERS: *(Weeping bitterly)* There must be some other explanation.

INSPECTOR HUFFINGTON: No. An examination of the body turned our suspicions into certainty.

SOUND: MRS. MALTRAVERS sobs

INSPECTOR HUFFINGTON: I'm employed by insurance company, what can I do? The evidence is conclusive.

SOUND: more sobbing

INSPECTOR HUFFINGTON: Madam, you of all people should know that there are no dead!

MRS. MALTRAVERS: What do you mean?

INSPECTOR HUFFINGTON: Have you ever taken part in a spiritualistic seance?

MRS. MALTRAVERS: Yes. I do seances.

INSPECTOR HUFFINGTON: Ah! You have the seeing eye, then?

MRS. MALTRAVERS: Well, I am mediumistic, that's true. With extrasensory perception.

INSPECTOR HUFFINGTON: Me too, madam, too me.

DENBY: Really, Huffy. You believe in this psychic stuff?

INSPECTOR HUFFINGTON: Yes. I have an open mind.

DENBY: Table levitation and all that? Bunch of mumbo-jumbo to me.

INSPECTOR HUFFINGTON: Well, didn't you hear what the gardener said?

DENBY: No, I missed that. What?

INSPECTOR HUFFINGTON: He said that Marsdon Manor is haunted.

DENBY: Haunted?

INSPECTOR HUFFINGTON: Aye.

GARDENER: Sure, sure. I've seen some strange things.

MRS. MALTRAVERS: Well, servants will gossip.

SOUND: scream from outside

GARDENER: It's a man — standing in the passage.

SOUND: footsteps rushing out

INSPECTOR HUFFINGTON: There's no one here.

GARDENER: Isn't there, sir? Oh, it gave me a start.

INSPECTOR HUFFINGTON: But why?

GARDENER: I thought — I thought it was the master — it looked like Mr. Maltravers.

SOUND: three raps

MRS. MALTRAVERS: Inspector Huffington, did you hear that? Those three taps on the window?

INSPECTOR HUFFINGTON: Are you thinking of the old superstition? That a suicide cannot rest?

MRS. MALTRAVERS: That's how he always used to tap, when he passed round the house.

DENBY: The ivy. It was the ivy against the pane.

MRS. MALTRAVERS: I hear footsteps.

DENBY: It's the wind. I'll close the door. And lock it.

MRS. MALTRAVERS: But this door is bewitched! Don't lock it.

SOUND: key locks a door

MRS. MALTRAVERS: *(Gasping)* Don't do that. If it comes open—

INSPECTOR HUFFINGTON: Madam, I have a bizarre suggestion. You are a medium? Perhaps you could get through to Jack. He could tell you what happened.

MRS. MALTRAVERS: Allright. I'll light the candles.

INSPECTOR HUFFINGTON: Thank you. Denby, draw chairs around this table, if you would.

DENBY Certainly.

INSPECTOR HUFFINGTON: And be quiet. Don't say a word. No matter what you hear or see.

MRS. MALTRAVERS: Jack? Jack? Can you hear me, Jack? Can you hear me? If you can, rap. Rap three times.

SOUND: three raps

MRS. MALTRAVERS: Listen, what was that? The front door slammed.

DENBY: No, Mrs. Maltravers, it was the thunder.

SOUNDS: door swings open, then MRS. MALTRAVERS shrieks

MRS. MALTRAVERS: There! In the doorway. I saw my husband. You must've seen him too.

INSPECTOR HUFFINGTON: Madam, I saw nothing. You are not well.

MRS. MALTRAVERS: I'm perfectly well. It was Jack, my husband. He pointed at me.

SOUND: lights dim

MRS. MALTRAVERS: The lights went out.

SOUND: three loud raps

MRS. MALTRAVERS: My God, there he is! *(Moans)* Jack, with blood on his lips.

DENBY: Huffy, look! Look at her hand. Her right hand. It's all red!

MRS. MALTRAVERS: Blood!

SOUNDS: MRS. MALTRAVERS goes into a trance, then collapses on the floor

MRS. MALTRAVERS: Yes, it's blood. I killed him. I killed Jack. I did it. He was showing me, and then I put my hand on the trigger and pressed. Save me from him — save me! He's come back!

INSPECTOR HUFFINGTON: Lights.

SOUND: lights warm up

INSPECTOR HUFFINGTON: That's it. You heard, Denby?

DENBY: Good Heavens. That lovely creature, a murderess.

INSPECTOR HUFFINGTON: Oh, by the way, this is Mr. Everett. Rather fine member of the theatrical profession. I phoned Mr. Everett this afternoon. His make-up is good, isn't it? Quite like a dead man. I wouldn't touch her right hand if I were you, Denby. Red paint marks so.

MRS. MALTRAVERS: You put red paint on my hand?

INSPECTOR HUFFINGTON: The color of blood.

MRS. MALTRAVERS: When? In the dark?

INSPECTOR HUFFINGTON: Yes. When the lights went out, I clasped your hand, you see.

MRS. MALTRAVERS: Oh.

INSPECTOR HUFFINGTON: Captain Black's story — it suggested an ingenious method of committing murder.

MRS. MALTRAVERS: No more. Please stop.

DENBY: What are you talking about, Huffy?

INSPECTOR HUFFINGTON: You don't see? Even now?

DENBY: Not quite, no.

INSPECTOR HUFFINGTON: To shoot himself, you see, he'd have to pull the trigger with his toe. If Mr. Maltravers had been found with one boot off, I'd be inclined to view this case as suicide, not murder. But I have no proof in support of my theory. Hence the elaborate little comedy you saw played tonight.

DENBY: Well, she could've fooled me.

INSPECTOR HUFFINGTON: Me too. If only she had taken off his shoe.

DENBY: Ah.

INSPECTOR HUFFINGTON: Yes, now let's start at the beginning. Here is a shrew. A scheming woman. She knows of her husband's financial debacle. She's tired of her elderly mate, who she just married for the money. She induces him to insure this life for a large sum.

DENBY: Huh.

INSPECTOR HUFFINGTON: Most women make a pretense of mourning their husbands, but not her. I've never seen such heavily-rouged eyelids!

DENBY: I did not observe them.

INSPECTOR HUFFINGTON: As always, Denby, you see nothing!

MRS. MALTRAVERS: Please stop talking.

INSPECTOR HUFFINGTON: The poor fool — he showed you. He placed the end of the gun in his mouth. You stooped down and put your finger on the trigger, laughing at him. And then — and then — you pulled it!

SOUNDS: distant gun shot, then theme music

End of Play

PLAYOGRAPHY

Mark Sbani Junior
Lincoln Center
New York City, New York
August 23rd, 2025

Mark Sbani Junior
George Bruce Public Library
New York City, New York
August 2nd, 2025

Mark Sbani Junior
Three Leaches Theatre
Lakewood, Colorado
August 2nd, 2025

Mark Sbani Junior
Mercury Cafe
Denver, Colorado
June 7th, 2025

Stand Up, Malvo!
Exposed Theatre
Denver, Colorado
May 1st, 2025

Oprah Hugs
Equity Library Theatre
New York City, New York
August 8th, 2024

Ten Stages of Love
The Secret Theatre
New York City, New York
February 25th — March 20th, 2024

Eigg the Musical
(book-writer)
Riddle's Court at Greenside
Edinburgh, Scotland
August 4th—12th, 2023

The Cold Facts
Kinda Vague Radio
Denver, Colorado
April 2nd, 2023

Ghost of Union Station
The Hypnotic Turtle Radio Circus,
KVCU 1190AM
Boulder, Colorado
October 31st, 2022

Alley Cat
Coffee Contrails Podcast
San Jose, California
June 28th, 2021

Born Fool
Tech Social
Denver, Colorado
June 30th, 2017

Blue Bear
(co-writer)
Time Capsule Framing
Denver, Colorado
April 1st, 2017

A Cure for the Drunken Heebie-Jeebies
Crossroads Theatre
Denver, Colorado
August 29th, 2014

Dr. Jekyll and Mr. Hyde
(adaptation)
Theatre-Hikes Colorado
Boulder, Denver, Chatfield, Chautatauqua, Cherokee Castle
August 5th—September 2nd, 2013

Bored to Death
Vintage Theatre
Denver, Colorado
December 21st—December 31st, 2011

AWARDS

Rocky Mountain Theatre Association,
"Best Full-Length Play,"
Shoeshine Girl, 2011

Broadway World Denver,
"Best New Musical,"
Eigg the Musical, 2023

Broadway World Denver,
"Best Musical,"
Eigg the Musical, 2023

Equity Library Theatre,
New York City,
"Special Mention Award,"
Oprah Hugs, 2024

Equity Library Theatre,
New York City,
"Best Performance, Monologues at Lincoln Center,"
Mark Sbani Junior, 2025

ARTWORK

Ten Stages Of Love

Sam Wick & Mark Sbani

Malvo Hill

Sam Wick

Ghost Of Union Station

Raymundo Munoz

The Tragedy At Marsdon Manor

Sam Wick

Self Portrait

Mark Sbani

DESIGN

Sam Wick

THANK YOU

Rob Dixon, Andrew Tallent, Sam Wick, Cathie Beck, Marissa Leotaud, Little Fyodor, Perry B. Anthony, Jon Sayles, Dave Colberg, Arlo White, Michael Lauter, Julia Huff, Jay Philly, Me Mum, Tony Savaglio, Joe D'altilia, Christin Mason, Dan Butcher, Ryan Hartley, Snezhana Chernyavskaya, Josh Shellman, Megan Wilt, Aaron Young, Monica Dionysiou, Suri Duitch, Chris Eller, Raymundo Munoz, Adam Leech, Kelly Jo Eldredge, Betc, Vintage Theatre, Edinburgh Fringe Festival, Equity Library Theatre, Savoy Theatre, R.r.c.c, Exposed Theatre, Josie Dixon, Antigone Biddle, Gary Johnson, Sarah Underbrink, Denver Fringe Festival, Savannah Mares O'Neill

MARK SBANI is a Denver playwright in his mid-40s, with short declarative hair, question mark-like eyebrows and a squiggly forehead. At age 29, he retired to the quiet lakes around Washington Park. He likes the flowers (nature's perfume) but not the geese (fat and disagreeable). Said Sbani: "Writing a play is like strangling a goose. It takes a long time."

www.ingramcontent.com/pod-product-compliance
Lightning Source LLC
LaVergne TN
LVHW010935110826
845149LV00013B/2611

* 9 7 9 8 9 9 8 7 9 4 9 0 2 *